Lighthouse
on the
Prairies

THE STORY INSIDE
THE JESUS ELEVATOR

HENRY VANDERPYL

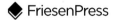

FriesenPress

Suite 300 - 990 Fort St
Victoria, BC, V8V 3K2
Canada

www.friesenpress.com

ISBN
978-1-9992807-0-3 (Hardcover)
978-1-9992807-1-0 (Paperback)
978-1-9992807-2-7 (eBook)
978-1-9992807-3-4 (Spiral Bound)

1. BIOGRAPHY & AUTOBIOGRAPHY, PERSONAL MEMOIRS

Distributed to the trade by The Ingram Book Company

Henry Vanderpyl

www.henryvanderpyl.com

403-360-6951

Table of Contents

ACKNOWLEDGEMENTS

Writing a book is not just a one-person task. I want to start this acknowledgement by thanking all those who ever said a prayer for me both before and after I decided to follow Jesus Christ. Some of whom, I don't even know their names.

I especially want to thank my six children; each of them expired (spell-check 'inspired') me in their own ways (and put up with my Dad jokes). I thank the Lord for my late wife, Mary Anne, who stood by me, loved me, and helped me to better understand what my focus in life should be. She set the stage for me to write this book.

I benefitted from a writer's retreat in 2019, hosted by Mark Buchanan who helped me to understand and refine the process of writing. At that retreat, I met Jared Seitz. Thank you, Jared, for your ongoing editorial assistance and wordsmithing. You helped me to correlate my random thoughts and encouraged me to expand my horizons.

I am particularly thankful to the various pastors and friends who encouraged me to complete this project. I choose not to list them here; they already know that appreciation is more than just listing names in calligraphy on a certificate of appreciation. Legacy can be eternal. I pray for them that their journeys in life will also be blessed.

Most of all, I thank Jesus for dying on the cross to make it possible for me to be forgiven and to have an eternal hope. God's words are life to them that find them and health to all their flesh. (see Proverbs 4:22)

FOREWORD

In 2014, praying and fasting, I was directed to Amos 8:11-12.

> "Behold, the days are coming," says the Lord GOD, "That I will send a famine on the land, Not a famine of bread, Nor a thirst for water, But of hearing the words of the LORD. They shall wander from sea to sea, and from north to east; they shall run to and fro, seeking the word of the LORD, but shall not find it. – (Amos 8:11-12 NKJV)

That is when I realized we are in a famine of hearing the words of the Lord. As I read Henry's book, I was reminded of the importance of reading the Bible on a regular basis. That it is alive and powerful.

This book will motivate you to be revived in reading and hearing the Word of God. This is a "now" book. It will fill you with spirit and life. This book is written to provide a balanced and practical life application of a central Bible principle that may become yours. This book will strengthen the power of the Word of God in your life.

Pastor Frank Harms
Founding Pastor
Revival Of Canada Christian Ministries
Coaldale, Alberta, Canada

INTRODUCTION

I Volunteered to be on a Swing Scaffold?

Sixty-five feet up, standing on a makeshift swing scaffold, I watched the traffic entering the city of Edmonton. Though hundreds of vehicles were passing every minute, I could never have imagined the impact nineteen wooden words—hammered into the face of an old grain elevator—were going to have.

You don't necessarily recognize the extent of what Jesus has done in your life until you start to write about it.

Since the time I could read and write, I have been an avid note-taker. I make notes for the future. I make notes for inspiration. Some of these notes (a lot of these notes), inspire calligraphy projects—some bigger than others.

Calligraphy—the art of free-hand lettering—started as a hobby for me. I can hardly connect the lines of a stick-figure, but, for whatever reason, I am able to draw lines into letters, letters into words—in such a way you would believe I pulled it from a printer. In fact, my sloppier work usually receives higher praise because it is recognized as hand-drawn, human-made art. People often ask me to write poems and sayings in my *Olde English* calligraphic style. Though I accept other tasks from time to time, I much prefer rewriting Bible verses.

Since the Jesus Elevator towered over the south entrance into Edmonton—"The Gateway to the North"—I have fought endlessly to keep the Word of God visible in my life. We may think we're not influenced, but unless we are diligent in our walk, even the most well-versed Christians might miss God's calling in their lives.

I have asked many people, believers or not, "When was the last time you saw God's Word, such as 'The Lord's Prayer' on public display?" The answer I hear most often: "*A long time.*"

God's commandments used to be on public display in most government buildings, court houses, libraries, and city halls. Schools were not in session until they finished reciting the Lord's Prayer. Scripture—a part of our Canadian heritage—was displayed with passion and purpose. Bit by bit, fewer and fewer testimonies of God's truth have been displayed in our homes, buildings (churches included)—and land.

To clarify, this book is not an attack against people who choose not to display the Word of God.

Since the demolition of the Jesus Elevator in 1989, a *trend* has been on the rise. In writing this book, my hope is not only to address this trend, but to encourage a new one: a *visible* resurgence of scripture—and not just in Edmonton, Alberta, but anywhere God sees fit. All Scripture is given by inspiration of God, and His word—sharper than any two-edged sword[1]—will not return void.

Reading (and re-reading) God's Word is never a waste of time: the *love* we receive in John 3:16; the *promise* made in Isaiah 55:11; the *worship* sung in Psalm 138:2. We serve an awesome God who loves us so much, he not only gave His one and only

---

1 See Hebrews 4:12

Son, he provided a complete operator's manual, the Holy Bible, so we might live life to the full. In following Jesus and surrendering myself to His word, I, for one, am ready to face eternity. In the meantime, I have promised Him, my wife Mary Anne, and my six children, to be the best *operator* I can be.

The Great Commission—to go into the world and spread the Good News—was spoken to every one of us; and, despite how insignificant we think they may be; we all have talents that God can *and intends* to use.

As you read—and because anything worth doing is worth doing with notes—I encourage you to write down the verses that speak to you—calligraphy optional. Just like your smartphone, feel free to also check your Bible throughout the day for new messages. You will be amazed how God designed your brain to retain His word. And, once you do, some more *good news* is that you will be able to share it with fellow believers, unbelievers, and travellers, far and wide, and—without having to look at your notes.

Something this good, this life-changing, should be shared. And that's exactly what the owner of the Jesus Elevator, Hartley Somerville, and I did.

CHAPTER 1

GO BIG OR GO HOME

Author's Background

My name is Hendricus (call me Henry) Vanderpyl (pro-nounced *Vander-pile*). I was blessed with almost forty years of marriage to a wonderful, godly woman, Mary Anne. Mary Anne passed away in 2017. Her loss, as any widower knows, was devastating at the time, and still is, to this day. It is by faith that I carry on, fighting the good fight while God has me here. Together, Mary Anne and I have six children.

I don't so much like the word *retirement*, and, achieving the age of sixty-eight at the time of writing, I am continuing to work and be in good health.

I was born in the spring of 1952 in Rotterdam, Netherlands. The greatest natural disaster to occur in the Netherlands in the 20th century began on January 31, 1953 and continued into February 1,1953. A major storm hit the Dutch coast with a combination of severe north-westerly gales in the North Sea, and a sea level surge of four to five metres above the average sea level.

> *The dykes were unable to cope with the volume of water and succumbed in more than 150 places in Zeeland, Zuid Holland, and Noord-Brabant, with disastrous consequences. On Sunday afternoon, residents were shaken by a second storm surge that caused even more casualties than the first. The flood took the lives of 1,836 people. More than 72,000 people were evacuated, 47,000 cattle and 140,000 poultry drowned. More than 150,000 hectares of land was inundated, causing severe damage to infrastructure and farmland. The natural disaster destroyed 4,300 houses and other buildings and damaged 43,000 more. The total cost of the damage was 1.5 billion guilders (the equivalent of 5.4 billion euro in today's money).*

(Ref: https://www.rijkswaterstaat.nl/english/water/water-safety/the-flood-of-1953/index.aspx accessed Sept. 19, 2019)

We lived in Rotterdam, which was partially affected by the flooding. Dad was born and raised in the Netherlands and had been trained as a professional baker and pastry chef. Mom was born and raised in East Germany and had moved to the Netherlands at the end of WW2. It was not easy for my mother, being German, to live in the Netherlands post-war. Not seeing much of a future in the Netherlands, my parents made the decision to take their four kids and emigrate to Canada. At fourteen months old, I was the youngest child. We arrived in Canada on June 30th, 1953, the day before "Dominion Day". (July 1st became a significant date for me; it has been called "Canada Day" since 1982.)

Our east coast landing at Pier 21 in Halifax was followed by a four-day train ride from the lighthouses of the Maritimes to the western limits of the prairies, arriving in Calgary, Alberta. My dad, a baker by trade, built a bakery in northwest Calgary alongside the Trans-Canada No. 1 highway, and he called it "Montgomery Bakery."

Dad had a talent for sketching and painting signs. He lettered the signage on the delivery vehicles by hand, and he painted a six-plywood-sheet sign on the side of the bakery, which read: *Last Bakery Before Banff.* I watched for hours while he designed and painted these signs. It was fascinating to see how many sheets of plywood with various hand-drawn words could be fitted together to produce such a pleasing display of art.

Four days before my eighth birthday, my younger sister was born. I thought that was a neat gift because now I wasn't the baby of the family. My parents, brother, and now three sisters, and I lived upstairs, and the bakery—and all its creations—was downstairs. For a decade Montgomery Bakery was a successful business.

One day, my oldest sister, Paula, discovered a Sunday school in a small Missionary Church half a block from the bakery. Mom said we could go, and—getting a much-needed break—sent us regularly for over a year. It was the only church I attended during childhood. We spent enough time to learn a few stories, a couple of songs, and most importantly, that *Jesus Loves Me.* I don't remember the name of my Sunday school teacher, but I remember that she made the stories interesting.

Other than a bit of Sunday school at age 9 to 10, I didn't have a church background. My Mom was from East Germany, and my Dad was from the Netherlands. As a family, we did not attend any church; most Saturday nights and Sundays were for camping. In grade five, I received a Gideons New Testament and—knowing it was something worth keeping, I—tucked it away.

Before Mom's fortieth birthday, my siblings and I pooled our money and bought a stainless-steel cooking pot for Mom—something we thought she always wanted. But, on her birthday, Mom was nowhere to be found. Outside our back door, large tracks and the imprints of two suitcases had made their marks in the snow. I followed the boot-prints, but—where they ended, tire marks began.

Mom was gone.

Was it something we had done? —Did we pick the wrong pot for her present?—And was Dad angry with us, or with Mom?

We were not receiving any clear answers. Instead, we were left to assume the worst, and likewise, experienced the same in return: "Don't have anything to do with Henry," other moms would say. "He's from a broken home." It was 1963. Broken families were uncommon—and *uncommon*—was *unaccepted*. People did not understand what happened to our family, and neither did I.

The following winter, a man from the Salvation Army visited the bakery, looking for corporate donations. Dad saw it as an opportunity to share his problems, and the guy quickly realized he wouldn't be getting a donation.

I was not looking forward to that first, broken Christmas: sitting by our decorated tree, eating shortbread cookies, singing songs, and opening presents—it all seemed pointless.

A few days before Christmas, there was a knock on our back door. Someone from the Salvation Army was dropping off a hamper. It was full of goodies, including snack-sized boxes of Sultana raisins. We had plenty of raisins in the bakery, but for whatever reason, the small, gift-wrapped boxes were more of a treat.

I don't remember the presents I got that year, but I'll never forget that hamper. It brightened our whole Christmas. Whenever I see someone wearing a Santa hat during a Salvation Army kettle campaign, I can't help but give him an extra reason to ring his bell and throw a bit of money his way. I know the seemingly small act goes a long way.

Doing good and loving others is a lot like making raisins. You may not see the transformation taking place, but, when we stay under the *Son*, walking in his holy ways, it doesn't take long before we're changed forever. And I once thought wrinkles were a bad thing.

Dad worked long hours and spent a lot of what little free time he had telling strangers about his problems. I remember one time, hungry and lonely, walking downstairs and peeking around the corner into the bakery. Though I was greeted by the smell of delicious stew, Dad didn't notice me. He was heating up a can of stew to feed his hunger—his needs. He had forgotten that I needed supper too. I tried to not hold these sorts of things against him, and if I did, I have forgiven him by now. Nevertheless, I knew my heart was hardening towards him, and life in and above Montgomery Bakery.

We saw Mom every couple of months—usually when Dad was doing deliveries. I stayed with my Dad for the next 3 years. My older siblings moved on and my little sister was boarded out somewhere with another family. I was not allowed to know where she was. Dad did not want Mom to get custody of her. Dad would often tell customers he couldn't wait until I was old enough to drive the delivery van, but Mom wanted me to finish school. I didn't know who I wanted to be yet, but deciding between being a delivery man and finishing high school, I was inclined toward further education.

At the time, though, neither option excited me much. I was searching for something money and intelligence couldn't buy. A quiet kid with a calm demeanor, I never had much trouble sleeping, but I would often lie in bed processing thoughts. Could Dad—seemingly incapable of processing his own problems—ever be able to take care of mine? …Maybe, I thought, love was something only promised in a Sunday school song.

In 1966, midway through grade eight, I left Dad and the bakery to live in Edmonton with Mom and my soon-to-be stepdad. I didn't want Dad to charge Mom with kidnapping, so I made it as clear as six sheets of plywood: *I, Henry Vanderpyl, am running away…*

Fourteen, annoyed, and ready to be on my own, I set a goal to finish high school, get a well-paying job, and—most importantly—have nothing to do with my parents.

My parents cared about me, but it would be many years before I'd experience feelings of true love that I missed during my childhood. Speed limits are slower in playground zones because children don't perceive traffic the way adults do. Similarly, children may seem resilient, but those coming from a broken home need all the spiritual help and prayer support they can get.

Processing a family break-up and the ongoing consequences takes years—and for some, a book.

A Centennial Project Worth Doing

When Canada celebrated its hundredth birthday in 1967, I knew I wanted to commemorate the milestone.

I thought about doing a coin collection, but for something as significant as the centennial, coins seemed a little standard—a little lame. "It should mean something," I thought, "and it should be a once-in-a-lifetime project." Then I got the idea to read the Bible cover to cover. After all, that was surely something you would only do *once* in your life.

I managed to find a full Bible (I still had only a travel-sized new testament), put it beside my bed, and began reading a few verses before falling asleep each night. I started in Genesis, the beginning of the book, made my way into Exodus, and eventually, it seems

I couldn't fall asleep faster if I tried. At this rate, my centennial project was going to require more than one lifetime.

Canadian Army Primary Reserves

In 1968, sixteen years old, I joined the Canadian army primary reserves as a member of the Loyal Edmonton Regiment (L.E.R.). A friend of mine was part of their reserve unit and invited me to join. "I'll at least get to shoot a gun, if nothing else," I thought. My mother did not like the idea, but figured it would be another fad, like tie-dye T-shirts. It wasn't. Two years later, and through consistent hard work, I held the rank of Corporal.

In October 1970, Canada was in crisis when the F.L.Q. (Front de Libération du Québec) kidnapped provincial Minister of Labour, Pierre Laporte and British diplomat, James Cross. This event was preceded by numerous bombs detonating in the mail, as well as the 1969 bombing of the Montreal Stock Exchange, which caused extensive damage and injured twenty-seven people. Stealing several tons of dynamite from industrial sites and the army, the well-supplied FLQ continued to bomb Montreal, targeting City Hall, the RCMP, and even military recruiting centres. They killed Pierre Laporte seven days after he was kidnapped.

Revolutionary anarchy was at our door, and with every knock, Quebec and the rest of Canada quivered with greater fear. Prime Minister Pierre Elliot Trudeau took action invoking the one and only use of the War Measures Act during peacetime in Canadian history. This gave the federal government greater police powers and the ability to overrule individual rights. This also put the army reserves into active service training for potential call-up to active duty.

During infantry tactics at Camp Wainwright, we had our standard FN rifles (the first semi-automatic weapon to be adopted by the Canadian Army), and 9-mm sub-machine guns—all with blank ammunition. Just before our training started, we were told the officer on a nearby hill had live ammo and was standing guard "in case certain terrorist elements try to ambush us for our weapons." If we hadn't been before, we were certainly standing at attention now. The armed officer on that hill remained a visual reminder for me and the other reservists to keep our eyes, ears—and prayer lines—open.

The FLQ is but one example of what can happen when evil finds its foothold. As Canadians, we might think we are free of terrorism: that evil is something lurking outside the borders of our provinces and territories. We can sing about it all we want: to stand on guard for Thee, to, alongside God, keep our land, true, strong and free, but to do so with *live* ammunition in our hearts—and at the tip of our tongues—that is something we must train for every day.

One recruit drove us crazy during training. He was always talking, and seldom paid attention to instruction. In shooting practice, everyone tried to get a spot as far away from him as they could. I felt bad for him—until the day he had us running for cover, breathing through our shirts, trying to escape the phosphorus smoke grenade fumes he accidentally unleashed.

"Don't release the grenades too early," our lieutenant reminded us again and again. So, what did *Yackety McYackerson* do?[2] His disobedient arm—yet to pass parallel to his shoulders—released the phosphorus smoke grenade just as he started to throw it, and we didn't stand a chance. It went sideways, landing beside our bunker instead of on the other side of the reinforced concrete bunker wall. Due to the wind direction, only a small cloud of phosphorus smoke engulfed us but some of us over-dramatized the coughing that ensued.

---

2   actual name protected for soldier's privacy

Throughout the F.L.Q. turmoil, I continued working on my centennial project. I didn't think it would help me look cool, reading the Bible, so I never brought it during summer and weekend training. Nevertheless, the limited reading during these years helped me understand there is more to life than what you hear through news and off-the-cuff (and sometimes inebriated) opinions of your peers.

Good friends, however, (inebriated or not) can often serve as lights in the darkness.

One night, to celebrate a couple of successful weeks of training, our group of twelve or so newly graduated non-commissioned officers were given a keg of beer. Everything—I've been told—tastes better when it's free. I drank lots that evening and was too drunk to stagger back to the barracks. One of my friends offered to drive me, and even stopped part way so I could lean out the passenger side and barf: liquid proof of the fun time I had. My friend was thankful I had the sense to leave the souvenir outside his car... the coming hangover was going to provide enough memory for a lifetime.

When we got to the barracks, he dropped me off twenty feet from the door and asked if I needed help getting inside. 'I see the door,' I said. 'I'm okay from here.' He drove off and I stumbled on. The next thing I remember is waking up in my bottom bunk, feeling as stiff as the boards supporting the bed above me. Rolling over, I told one of my buddies I felt like I had been thrown into bed. His response: "Yeah, you were passed out in the hallway, so I picked you up and put you in your bunk."

That scared me.

I couldn't remember going through the door, let alone being tucked-in by a full-grown man. How can I stand on guard for Thee when I can't even stand on my own two feet? I was thankful for my friends—they were decent guys—but I couldn't believe the blinding power we exposed ourselves to through alcohol. From that day on, and at the cost of a few friendships, I promised I would never drink in excess again.

I stayed with the Loyal Edmonton Regiment until 1971, then transferred to the Royal Canadian 8th Field Engineers until '73, earning the rank of 2nd Lieutenant.

While part of me still longed for the thrill promised at the bars, something told me I was on the wrong path. Believing it was my better self calling for help, I listened to that voice. Little did I know people were praying for me at this time.

It is your direction, not your intention, that determines where you are going. I didn't yet know where I was headed, but I was determined to not only make it back to my bunk from that day forward, but to craft—carefully—a life worth living. A life that, had it not been for God's Word, other people's prayers, choosing to go to college and university, and of course—meeting Mary Anne—would not have taken place.

CHAPTER 2
THE SCHOOL OF CALLIGRAPHY

Before college, I attended Queen Elizabeth Composite High School in Edmonton. The school motto is *Virili Parte*, meaning: *To the Utmost of Our Ability*.

The school didn't have a shop facility, so without the opportunity to take automotive shop or woodworking, I signed up for typing and drafting.

Typing, as it turned out, was a timely-acquired skill. I learned a lot from the teacher, Mr. Hank Kalke. He took time explaining why documents were formatted the way they were, and there was something about his demeanor—it was clear that he genuinely cared for each of his students.

In grade ten Drafting class, we learned to use old-fashioned ink pots and metal Speedball™ pen nibs, which needed constant dipping and re-dipping in ink. We felt like scribes of the Middle Ages. Our teacher, Mr. Mikytyshyn, patiently taught us how to

hold our pens and print different styles—all by hand, of course—
no stencils allowed.

I had a hard time developing a unique style and struggled with
slanted letters. Asking Mr. Mikytyshyn if I could do block printing
with vertical letters instead, he said, "Yes. That *is* a style." And so I
went: creating my own slantless *Vanderpyl-style*. Or, "Times New
Henry", if I were to give it a more casual name. I particularly liked
Olde English and was always tweaking the letters to make them
more readable.

Though somewhat archaic, the old methods taught us many
required skills: consistency, topping them all. The Speedball™ nibs
were made of several layers of metal to make them flexible and retain
more ink. We quickly (and comically) discovered, if you didn't pull
the nib from top to bottom and left to right, you would bend its
tabs the wrong way and the nib would catch the fibres of the paper.
This resulted in a *twang*. Congratulations… you just sprayed the
back of the student in front of you. Or worse yet, depending on your
viewpoint, you might have sprayed your own drawing with ink that
is hard—if not impossible—to erase, and you'd have to start again.

Through trial and error, we learned to hold our pens correctly:
to make vertical strokes from top to bottom and horizontals from
left to right. Of course, if you were left-handed, the direction of
the pen could be modified, but should, nevertheless, be consistent.
Repetitive discipline: providing the basic skills for hand lettering
since the dawn of pictograms and stone slates. Can I get a:

3

---

3   I grew up watching The Flintstones cartoons on TV. This was Fred's modern,
stone-age expression of happiness and excitement. The voice-over for Fred
Flintstone's wife Wilma was done by Jean *Vanderpyl*—who is famous, but as far
as I know, not related to me.

During these introductory drafting classes, I also learned about line-weights, plan views, two and three-point perspectives, cross-sections, and how to carefully map out a presentation. Our class also earned the privilege to make posters for school events, and not falling too far from Dad's example, I gravitated towards larger posters:

Go Big or Go Home

[4]

The Role of a Civil Engineering Technologist

When I graduated in 1970, I felt a high school diploma was not enough to start a career—at least not one that would carry me into the next millennium. Though we still circled the sun in the same three hundred and sixty-five days, I felt the world was moving faster, and I wanted to be up to speed.

I thought about pursuing drafting. I also saw surveyors enjoying warm weather and thought it may be a nice career. (I was forgetting that outdoor jobs in Canada also meant a forty-degree swing, come winter.) And despite excelling in the reserves, I never thought of the army as my long-term solution to making a living. After writing a list of choices, crossing-out and writing them again, I decided my best career choice was to go to college at the Northern Alberta Institute of Technology (NAIT). I was deciding between Drafting Technology and Survey Technology, but when I found out Civil Engineering Technology offered courses in both drafting and surveying, my decision was made.

---

4   do whatever you are doing to its fullest, or, in my case, to its largest?

I entered with three years of drafting knowledge; nevertheless, NAIT would not give credit toward my basic drafting course. I fought the decision and lost. (*I was lettering all the time; I knew more than they did!*) My pens, always accessible in my shirt pocket, had become my instrument of choice, a way to show my talent and my worth. The ink, however, was starting to spray back on me.

The course required that we hand in one sheet of lettering each week. I did the first assignment carefully to show off what I could do. When the instructor handed it back, he told me not to bother with the weekly hand-ins. This helped disarm my attitude and I

ended up learning a lot and enjoying his class. Learning is so much more than being a good student: it's *wanting* to be a good student— and to the utmost of our ability.

I spent many hours scouring NAIT's library. On one visit, researching Olde English literature, I stumbled upon the word:

Wait a second; no one told me I was doing "Calligraphy!"

I had been practicing for four years without it having a name. This turned out to be a blessing in disguise since, had I known it was *a thing*, I would have researched it, and—through repetitive discipline—tried to master it, inside and out. Since I didn't know, I had to pull from my own creativity in developing a style. In professional calligraphy, the capital letters for "h" and "k" look almost the same as they do in lower case. Though I wanted to be a professional, I wanted a style that was easy to read—even if that meant "going against the fibers."

During my first year at NAIT, I helped with the annual open house event that showcased courses and programs for prospective students. Our rivals, the Architectural Technology students, always had artistic—pretty—models, and won themselves the open house trophy for best display—taking the title for the third year in a row.

The following year, I nominated myself to organize the Civil Tech display and compete for that trophy. My classmates and I—along with the visual aid of our cross-sectioned plywood model—demonstrated how a curved road is built. The grader, loader, and trucks were—of course—not true to scale, nor were the landscape components very pretty, but it did show—and in exemplary fashion, I might add—how a roadway is engineered.

The night before the open house, our team was setting up the displays between drinking bottles of beer. Late in the evening, with the display almost complete, we lacked one thing—we didn't have any signs or labels. Between beers, I asked them to write brief descriptions of each display so I could recreate them in my Olde English style.

A stack of notes was forming in front of me, so I didn't try to make each letter perfect like I usually did. (The two beer that I drank didn't help to keep things straight either.) We got them done, and all before *last call*, and learning from my previous experience, I did not drink any more beer to celebrate.

Doing calligraphy in the early 70s, people called me a monk; so I thought, why not do a five-foot-tall scroll to welcome everyone? I titled it, *The Role of the Civil Technologist*.

We put a lot of work into our display. "Coarse gravel overlaid by finer gravel, then asphalt," sounds simple, until you start reverse-engineering everything that goes into it.

In 1972, for the first time ever, Civil Tech received the NAIT Open House Trophy, and I was selected to receive it on our team's behalf. Hoisting it above my head, I snuck a sideways glance at the students in Architectural Technology, and they were—to my delight—disappointed. A historic rivalry exists between NAIT engineering and architectural technology students, which might be why, to this day, when someone comments on how beautiful a building is, I always say, "Yeah, can you imagine the engineering that went into it?"

My Friend Became a Jesus Follower

I graduated from NAIT with honours and enrolled at the University of Alberta to become a professional Civil Engineer. My best friend and NAIT classmate, Garry Stebner, also enrolled. Together, we occasionally went to the bar.

In the summer of '74, I worked in Fort McMurray as a junior inspector on a sewer, water, and roadway construction project. It didn't matter what day of the week it was, many of the workers on our site would be high on marijuana and/or alcohol while working. It was not a safe or pleasant place to work and I quit before the end of August. I phoned my previous employer the Friday before the September long weekend and was instantly re-hired (with a raise). To celebrate, I called Garry and asked if he'd join me at the bar for a couple drinks.

"I appreciate the offer, Henry, but I don't do that anymore," he said. "I've given my heart to Jesus."

The phone went silent for a few seconds, and then Garry continued by telling me how one of the rowdiest guys from NAIT, had given his heart to the Lord. After the call, I remember staring blankly at the phone. "Well, Garry's no fun anymore," I thought out loud. But secretly, the call left me contemplating... I wanted to know more.

A couple of weeks later, Garry called and invited me to church. He wanted to be friends, but whether or not I joined him at church, he wouldn't be joining me at the bar. "If you decide to come," he said, "don't come because I want you to; come because *you* want to."

I could tell he was sincere, and I thought about his call for three weeks.

Later, I found out Garry had been praying for me that summer, and was praying all the more since inviting me to church. What he didn't know was, I was still working on my centennial project, and I had been persistent in reading the Bible—on and off, and on again—for seven years. Though it wasn't easy, I even got through all of the Old Testament *begats* in the book of Chronicles, and some, more than once, as I kept losing my place.

Garry's new outlook on life surprised me, but, somehow, I sensed he was on the right path. I was reading Luke, Chapter 15 when I finally accepted his invitation.

I snuck into a pew near the back. It was a big church, seating over a thousand people. The pastor explained the gospel and invited anyone who did not have a personal relationship with Jesus to come forward. I looked down the long aisle and saw a foreman I didn't get along with. "What is he doing here?" I thought, wondering what ridicule I might be in for if he saw me answering the altar call. Though my fear of his opinion almost kept me in my seat, I decided in that moment to stop living for myself—no matter the cost. I forgave the man in my heart, and—as I passed by—realized it wasn't him. Life is full of hurdles. Sometimes, they are placed by our own hands—our own thoughts. God does that, or allows that, for a reason.[5]

Out of nowhere, Garry came forward and prayed for me and I accepted Jesus as my Lord. Life has never been the same.

---

5   Mark 11:24-25

There is joy in heaven over one sinner that repenteth.
– (see Luke 15:7 KJV) [6]

I continued reading my Bible and could not believe it was the same book. Before, I was reading about a man who did incredible things, died and came back to life, and did some more incredible things. Now, I was reading about my Lord and Saviour, Jesus, everything He did for me, and—being a sinner—how desperately I needed him.

Twenty-two years old, my only regret was not accepting Him sooner. I was following Jesus. No turning back. No running away.

Garry and I had traded invitations. I invited him to the bar; he invited me to church. But Garry also prayed. Prayer: an invisible billboard that compels the soul.

Believe it and Receive it.
– (derived from Mark 11:24) [7]

---

6 *This* was the first message on the Jesus Elevator.

7 Derived from Mark 11:24

CHAPTER 3

FROM ONE ALTAR TO ANOTHER

When I was in grade seven, it was mandatory to take music. *Doh-ray-me-fa-so-la-tea-doh*, though requiring repetitive discipline, was not for me, and—as you might guess—bad behaviour took hold. Eventually, Miss Fandry, the music teacher, had enough and sent me and two other boys to detention. We were to stay after school and sing for the Principal.

Like a scene from *The Sound of Music*, our impromptu trio was required to face the Principal and sing—unrehearsed—a little song. Miss Fandry played the piano while our Principal did a good job of keeping a straight face. It seemed to be going fine until, mid-chord, Miss Fandry abruptly stopped playing and asked, "What is that awful noise?"

I lip-synced after that.

Post altar-call, I was now attending church regularly. During praise and worship, the worship team repeated a hymn or song only once—twice if it was *really* good—and then they moved on to another. Ask anyone who has stood next to me during a rendition of *Happy Birthday*—singing is not my primary gift. But, I wanted to sing for Jesus: His praises, His name, and His love. The only song I knew was, coincidentally, "Jesus Loves Me."

Looking around that Sunday, the service packed full of adults in semi-formal attire, I thought, "They wouldn't sing that here..." The very next song: "Jesus Loves Me." I was so surprised, I immediately started singing along—*out loud*. God is good—and funny.

I read about water baptism in my Bible and I decided to get baptized. I simply made a quality decision, and I acted on that decision—I took God's Word seriously. I realized that water baptism is an outward symbol of my inward commitment. It indicates to others, our dedication to following, serving, and obeying Christ. So, I invited my Mom and stepfather to the baptism service. Why would we not want to share the most meaningful relationship with everyone around us, just as we would an engagement, a marriage, or the birth of a child? I don't think they had ever been in a church like that one.

Early in 1975, I thought about the pastor of the little Sunday school church I had attended for a short season in Calgary. For whatever reason, I felt I wanted to visit him. I drove three hundred kilometres from Edmonton to Calgary, walked up to the house where I thought he lived, and knocked on the door. A man opened the door, and I asked for Mr. Hertzsprung. "I am Mr. Hertzsprung," the man said, but he looked too young. I said, "The guy I'm looking for is a lot older than you," to which Irwin Hertzsprung responded: "Oh, that's my Dad, he lives next door."

The older Mr. Kaj Hertzsprung remembered all four of my siblings, asking about each of them by name, without me having to prompt him. Then he told me he had been praying for our family all these years. He was quite ill, and passed away just a few months after my visit.

For everyone who asks receives; the one who seeks finds;
and to the one who knocks, the door will be opened.
—*Luke 11:10 (NIV)*

I believe the idea for my centennial project came forth because Pastor Kaj Hertzsprung was praying for me. I believe God answers prayers. While some could only see our family as a problem, Pastor Kaj Hertzsprung saw us and our situation as an opportunity worth praying for—for twelve years. He even visited Dad at one point, trying to talk sense into him. (Biblically and sympathetically, I'm sure.)

I've never been good at remembering names. One tactic I've used at church is asking to see someone's Bible, hoping they had inscribed their identity on the flyleaf. So long as they weren't using somebody else's, it has helped me out of many potentially-awkward conversations.

At a Bible study, someone, (I forget their name), mentioned that you can find scripture references by looking up keywords in a concordance. A "concordance"—I never heard of such a thing. I learned that it was an alphabetical index of every word in the Bible, with references to the passages in which they occur. What an incredible resource.

It was fascinating to see all the study aids that were available. You know how exercise, at first, is grueling and exhausting? But, the more you do it, the easier and more enjoyable it becomes? Or maybe you don't exercise and don't plan to, but you're really good at something—were you always that good? The first time I held a crayon, I looked like I was preparing for a surprise attack. I wrote illegibly. I coloured outside the lines. I snapped crayons in half because I was pushing too hard. But, today, I hold a pen like I was always made to hold one.

Reading the Bible is like anything: it is hard until you love it. And once you learn to love it, you'll find that it is not boring, but interesting; not outdated, but relevant; not demanding, but loving; not belittling, but encouraging; not make-believe, but real, truthful, and wise.

After making Jesus the Lord of my life, I went to every Bible study I could. Church wasn't just a Sunday ritual; it was seven days a week. I didn't know much about the translations, denominations, and church protocols, but I was quickly learning *Christianese*—a whole new world of language and culture.

Attending every study and service also meant less time to complete my homework. So, to balance the school of life with the school of Christ, I decided to only go to some of the *extra* studies if my schoolwork was done.

One of the studies I attended was in Leduc, in the basement of a house where four single guys lived. I liked hanging out there, and, before long, I was moving in: Bachelor Number Five. I know, that sounds like the title for a blockbuster backslide, but I was done with the wrong kind of partying, and thankfully, so were they.

We pooled our resources to assist one of the guys, Allan McBryan, to work in full-time ministry—mostly at the University of Alberta. Though life beckoned, we all wanted to be involved in ministry. We called our fellowship group "On The Street Evangelistic Society" and even started a club at the university—we called it "One Way Agape"—to spread the good news.

With the club, we hosted several evangelistic events, bringing in Christian speakers qualified to debate Creation-Evolution.

Not wanting to be outdone by other clubs' advertising (and consistent with my tendency to make signs as big as the trees the paper was made from), I made a couple of extra-large posters to hang in the Central Academic Building, on the balconies so that people in the bottom floor cafeteria could read them while they ate their scrambled eggs. Using five-foot-wide newsprint rolls, I made posters fifteen by twenty feet in size. If there was a record book including the largest indoor poster sign on a university campus, I think there's a good chance it would still hold my name. A sample of the poster content:

"Coffin lays evolution theory to rest" – hear Dr. Harold Coffin, M.Sc. Zoology, Ph.D. Marine Biology

The poster included a drawing of a gravestone with "Evolution Theory R. I. P." and a statement that the "missing links" are still missing.

"From Fish … to Gish?"—hear Dr. Duane Gish, Ph.D. Biochemistry.

The poster included a sketch of an ape eating a banana, with the caption "Neanderthal Man—Our Father?" and a statement that evolution is scientifically bankrupt, creationism is scientifically sound. The fossils say NO to evolution. The fossils say YES to creationism.

CityJournal EDITOR: STEPHEN HUME

Bills
can be
real find

It was a windfall, money from heaven for university students lunching Thursday in the basement cafeteria of the Central Academic Building. Third-year commerce student Lonnie Homeniuk and others performed the Commerce Week Money Drop, showering bills down from the building's balconies while students below scrambled to share the wealth. Too bad all that phoney money was mixed in with the dollar bills!

PHOTOS BY
STEVE MAKKIS
JIM COCHRANE

|← 15 ft. →|

In the background of this photo is the top of the 15ft. x 25ft. poster hanging from the balcony.
(Source: Edmonton Journal news article, March 11, 1977 p.13)

Commuting from Leduc to the university every day of the week, I passed the grain elevator near Ellerslie, and read its painted scripture many times:

> Jesus said: There is joy in heaven over one sinner that repenteth. – Luke 15" [8]

As mentioned earlier, Luke 15 was the chapter I was reading before Garry's invitation to come to church. I found it all too easy to relate to the message. I was by no means a prodigal for reckless living, but I had run away and, in the process, hurt my dad. I had participated in excessive drinking, carousing, and foolish speech. I had put my needs ahead of the needs of others, and though I had been reading my Bible for years, I had nevertheless been set on walking *my* path, on *my* terms.

When I get to heaven, I would love to see a recording of the celebration they had when I gave my heart to Jesus. It was the 70's mind you... so they might only have it on VHS.

My Calligraphy Calling

A few weeks after becoming a Christian, I was out for a walk, praying by myself, and thanking Jesus for helping me and for expanding my circle of friends. I was enjoying the Bible studies and prayer meetings, but I longed for something more... something life-bringing. "I can't play any musical instruments," I thought. "I can't sing well or speak in front of crowds."

How could I have a ministry when there was nothing I could do? Then, almost audibly, I heard the question:

---

8   based on verses 7 & 10, KJV

What can you do?

To which I replied: I can do calligraphy... and that is what I did.

I started by writing people's names in their Bibles. It was simple, but it also meant something. Someone's name, given by their parents, is something precious. Connect it with something even more precious—the Bible—and we had a winning combination. And of course—it helped me with remembering names.

Writing names in Bibles led to people asking if I could write names for baptism certificates, certificates of appreciation, special occasion cards, and the like. I enjoyed doing that, but not as much as I enjoyed writing their favourite bible verse.

Penny, a girl from our Bible study, asked me to write her name in her new, *expensive* study Bible. She watched nervously as I wrote each letter of her name, praying—I'm sure—for me not to make a mistake. (Calligraphy—like anything—always turns out better if you pray first.) Penny, who incidentally also helped to educate me on cross-references and concordances, also insisted I mark and underline verses I found meaningful.

Later, Penny misplaced her Bible and was asking God for help finding it. She thought she had left it on the roof of her car and lost it while driving. When a construction worker came upon it, because it had her name written (legibly) in it, he was able to return it to her. She was overjoyed. I was encouraged. And my calligraphy ministry was just getting started.

Penny's Bible was valuable, not because it cost a pretty penny (yes, pun intended), but because it served as an instant connection to Christ.

Heaven rejoices when a sinner repents; and maybe, just maybe, two angels high-five when a Bible is found... one can dream, anyhow.

Psalm 91 Scripture Scroll

Penny lived in a basement suite in Leduc with two other girls who also attended the Bible studies. The owner of the house had installed vertical wood panelling throughout the suite. Every wall... Every cupboard... Panels. When a blind friend of theirs visited, he ran his fingers down the walls and commented on the monotonous design. If they didn't have confirmation before, they had it now.

Penny asked if I would write out a verse they could hang up to cover at least one of the sections of paneling. When I quizzed her on which verse she'd like, she said: "I won't tell you what I really want." But after she said that, I had to know, so I assured her that so long as it wasn't the entire begetting sequence from the book of Matthew, I was up to the task. Her answer: the entire chapter of Psalm 91, written out like a scroll.

I had wanted to do a scripture scroll, and readily agreed that Psalm 91 was an excellent choice. We measured one of the wall panels to be two feet wide and five and a half feet tall. Though I was taller, in my mind it towered over me. This was just one of the many calligraphy giants I was going to take on.

I told Penny I would do the scroll on good quality tracing paper, which would allow me to duplicate and distribute copies, and promised her the original.

Though it was an intimidating project, I was excited to get to work. I used India ink with Speedball™ pen nibs to write the verses. Writing the chapter turned out to be the easier part. But, the border, I thought, should be something special to complement the calligraphy. I couldn't decide on a suitable pattern, and began praying for inspiration.

For my first scroll at the NAIT open house (which was about the same size), I used a compass to create continuous linked curves in a chain-like effect for the border. After trying a few different chain-link designs, I discovered that a Christian fish symbol could be repeated in a similar way. I loved it, and decided on double lines to make it stand out more. Then the thought came to me to print Bible verses in a chain effect woven from the top of one fish to the bottom of the next, and so forth. I chose verses from the Bible which we sang as choruses during our Bible studies. The spacing was a bit of a challenge, but with a bit more trial and error, they all fit—perfectly.

I love singing verses taken from the Bible. It's a wonderful way to absorb God's Word and its life-giving, life-improving, life-sustaining message.

Finally, I used a match to (carefully) burn the edges, framing the piece within an uneven, rustic border.

My masterpiece; co-created with God's Word.

This is one of the Psalm 91 scrolls which were produced in 1975. It has been hanging on display for decades in a church located in Blackfalds, Alberta.

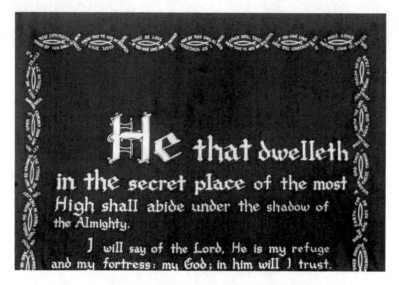

Close-up of the scroll border used for the various scrolls

I must admit, for a day or two after completing the project, I felt a bit like Sméagol from Lord of the Rings, arguing with my inner-Gollum. Giving up the original felt like giving up a child—or at least a well-behaved pet. But I could not deny the promise I made to Penny, and I wanted her to have it more than I wanted to keep it.

I proceeded to have the scroll photographically reduced to a more manageable size, 15 inches wide by 41 inches high, which would allow for easier reproduction and display.

I went to a specialty print shop with modern photographic reproduction equipment. The year was 1975, so it was camera with film, but their camera was large, mounted on rails and in its own room. They fed a massive roll of film into it (in a dark room) and produced a negative 15 inches wide by 41 inches long. From this negative, they produced a positive on acetate, clear plastic. This way I could run blueprints from either the negative or the positive to produce either white letters on a dark background, or dark letters on a white background.

It was an expensive process, but I wanted a few options to be able to produce multiple copies of the scroll on either blueprint or sepia paper. I also asked the shop to print a few full-size blueprints of the original.

A few weeks later, on my way to pick up the order, I was thinking about how much work had gone into the project and how excited I was to give Penny the original.

Then, a couple kilometers from the print shop, my heart sank into the seat of my pick-up. It was almost as if a passenger was sitting beside me, prematurely bursting my bubble. I don't know how I knew, but I did: the original, and every carefully placed pen stroke, had been destroyed.

I pulled into the parking lot in front of the shop and took a few minutes to catch my breath. Calm enough to speak, I entered and told the man at the counter I was there to pick up my Psalm 91 scroll and blueprints. "The scroll..." the man began, "We had some problems with your order, just a minute, and I'll go get it."

I know! my mind screamed. Had I not known already, my tongue would surely have jumped out of my mouth, climbed over the counter and proceeded to beat the man with every synonym I knew for *incompetent fool*.

He carried out the original in two diagonally-torn and wrinkled pieces.

"We're really sorry about this, sir," the man said. "The problem was—with the irregular burnt edges and the sheer length of the scroll, it was hard to feed it through our blueprint rollers... so it snagged and... well... you can see what happened..."

I had operated a blueprint machine on numerous occasions. I knew you had to watch how the originals went into the rollers. I knew if ever they started going through crooked, you needed to hit the reverse button and realign the feed. You waste a bit of paper, but you protect the original. Because I knew all this, I also knew: the machine didn't wreck the scroll—the operator did.

Fortunately, they had taken a full-scale photograph first, and were able to make a full-sized, clear, plastic reproducible print to enable future blueprinting. They also made some extra prints at no charge and reduced my total bill.

I listened quietly to all of this and looked at the prints which were well done.

"I would have preferred to have my original intact," I said, "but, that is obviously not possible... Nevertheless, I see you did everything you could to make up for it."

And with that, I paid my bill and left.

A year or two later, I was at a meeting where someone received a word of knowledge and prophesied a blessing on someone. "Wow," I thought. "But, God... where's my word of knowledge?" Then I remembered the scroll. Some call it intuition, but I know the truth: God gave me the heads up. Had He not, my reaction might have not only turned every worker at the shop away from the Bible, it might have given them a bad taste about God. I wouldn't want that—and more importantly—neither did God.

God will give you what you need—when you need it—as you trust and serve Him. Psalm 91 says it better. If you'd like to open up your Bible and read it, sing it, or sing and dance to it, do it now—I'll wait.

Back to the Altar

It was October 20, 1974 when I accepted Jesus as my Lord. That fall, I received a Christmas card from a girl named Mary Anne. Our families knew each other through mutual friends in the southern-Alberta Dutch community. I responded to her with a letter explaining how I had accepted Jesus and was celebrating my first Christmas as a born-again Christian. For our first date, we went to a basketball game. I can't recall who was playing or what the score was—I didn't care—I was with Mary Anne, the prettiest girl there.

A few weeks later, she invited me to go to a Berean Bible College preview weekend. One problem: she was so popular; she went out with another guy that weekend. My competitive spirit was lit, and I worked hard to spend as much time with Mary Anne as I could. When she asked me to escort her to her high school graduation in June of '75, I was so honoured, my face could not hide the pride inside as every jealous guy looked our way.

Mary Anne and I continued dating and, by Christmas, I was ready to propose. Truly, I was ready to propose the previous Christmas—the minute I laid eyes on her—but Dutch dating tradition isn't just splitting the bill; it's making sure you're compatible for life.

We were engaged for a year and four months before marrying. I was completing my studies in Edmonton while she was at college in Red Deer. That meant I spent a lot of time commuting back and forth on the Queen Elizabeth II Highway. Driving the "Queen" to visit my queen—worth every second and every ounce of fuel spent. While working part-time, Mary Anne earned a one-year Rehabilitation Services Certificate.

For a chance to join her on a summer missions program with Global Outreach Mission in 1976, I sold my truck. I liked that truck, but I would have given up a kidney if it meant spending the summer with Mary Anne.

Global Outreach selected teams for each country and I was honoured (and relieved) to be able to go on the same team as Mary Anne, doing six weeks of outreach in the Netherlands. It would be my first time visiting the Netherlands, where I was born and spent the very first non-memory-forming year of my life. I had relatives there, but I did not have contact with them—nor did I know where they lived.

I had lost contact with my Dad and my younger sister. Dad did not want Mom to gain custody of my younger sister, so he disappeared with her. I wondered if perhaps Dad went back to the Netherlands.

Mary Anne always strived for us to dive into God's Word together, and before our trip, she bought me a new study Bible. Mary Anne knew: books can inform you—but only the Bible can transform you.

We sang at coffee café places (yes, I can sing somewhat if I put in the effort). We also went door-to-door in the city of Hilversum, which was our home base that summer. We also participated in a tent crusade in Middelburg, Netherlands, assisting a Baptist pastor. Twenty-four years old, I was one of the older members of the team, which included Mary Anne, three more Canadian girls, an American girl, and me as team leader. And, because I had an international driver's license, I was also our team's driver, which, in hindsight, worked well, as it can be a little hard to lead if you're not the one steering.

Joining a larger team of a dozen or so youths from the Netherlands, we paired up two at a time when going door-to-door. Whenever there was an odd number, I often went by myself. I could speak Dutch well enough to be understood, and most Netherlanders knew at least a bit of English.

After a Christ-centred conversation, we gave them free copies of the New Testament, along with booklets of the Gospel of John. The residents, who were mostly friendly and welcoming, told me the area was nicknamed *The Bible-Belt*. To my surprise, however, most homes didn't carry a Bible. Some homeowners said they would be inheriting their family's heirloom Bible when Grandma passed away, but for an area known as *The Bible-Belt*, it was surely experiencing a longstanding drought.

This experience created in me a burden and a never-ending desire to help God's people access the scriptures, and learn about Jesus. The trip was also a highlight in getting to know my fiancée.

Mary Anne and I were a team right from the beginning. We married on April 30th, 1977—the week after I graduated from the U of A—and I moved into her apartment in Red Deer, evicting her maid of honour in the process. For our honeymoon, we took a road trip to Disneyland (Anaheim, California) in Mary Anne's '66 Chevy. In 1979, Mary Anne completed her College Diploma in Rehabilitation Services, and continued to work in that field. She was extremely talented working with special needs people.

Our first Christmas was spent on a mission team outreach with Operation Mobilization, ministering in Saltillo, Mexico, sharing *The Jesus Film* in Spanish. Then we spent a couple of months in early 1978 at the Agape Force training school in Texas. We did door-to-door outreach; and enjoyed working together actively spreading the Good News.

For a couple of years, we were leaders of a young adult youth group called the 20-30 Fellowship, sharing life-changing scriptures with many people. During these years, I did a lot of good-news-calligraphy, which Mary Anne fully supported.

Corrie ten Boom, The Hiding Place

The true story of Corrie ten Boom is important to people of Dutch ancestry, as well as anyone who experienced the war. My father was turning twenty when Nazi Germany invaded the Netherlands on May 10, 1940. During the German occupation, the Nazis conscripted forced labour by rounding up Dutchmen who were old enough to work in factories supporting the German war infrastructure.

They evacuated and searched the area where my father lived and so, knowing it was too big a risk to leave, my dad spent several days hiding in the Biesbosch: a swampy area in South Holland. He was shot at by both the Nazis and Allied force liberators. Fortunately, he was able to surrender to the Allies. He was also able to provide them with information about German artillery placements that were disguised in residential buildings, which the Allied soldiers were then able to bomb.

Mary Anne's parents—who were also born in the Netherlands—were active in the Dutch underground during the war. They hid draft-evaders in their residence, narrowly escaping being caught. Though they went as far as facing interrogation by the Gestapo,[9] God was with them, and they came through okay.

It was fairly common for Netherlanders to be active in the Resistance. What was not considered common were the heroic acts of Corrie ten Boom who—not only forgave those who persecuted her—but those who tortured and killed members of her family.

Through 1943 and 1944, the ten Boom home in Haarlem, Netherlands was a refuge for Jews. Alas, the ten Boom family were betrayed, arrested by the Nazis, sent to prison and then to a concentration camp, where Corrie's father and sister both died. One week before all the women prisoners her age and older were exterminated, Corrie—by the grace of a clerical error—was released from Ravensbruck Concentration Camp.

---

9 The official secret police of Nazi Germany and German-occupied Europe.

After her release, she wrote a letter to the person who had originally revealed her family's work to the Nazi Germans:

Dear Sir,

Today I heard that most probably you are the one who betrayed me. I went through 10 months of concentration camp. My father died after 9 days of imprisonment. My sister died in prison, too.

The harm you planned was turned into good for me by God. I came nearer to Him. A severe punishment is awaiting you. I have prayed for you, that the Lord may accept you if you will repent. Think that the Lord Jesus on the Cross also took your sins upon Himself. If you accept this and want to be His child, you are saved for Eternity.

I have forgiven you everything. God will also forgive you everything, if you ask Him. He loves you and He Himself sent His Son to earth to reconcile your sins, which meant to suffer the punishment for you and me. You, on your part, have to give an answer to this. If He says, "Come unto Me, give Me your heart," then your answer must be, "Yes, Lord, I come, make me Your child." If it is difficult for you to pray, then ask if God will give you His Spirit, who works the faith in your heart.

Never doubt the Lord Jesus' love. He is standing with His arms spread out to receive you.

I hope that the path which you will now take may work for your eternal salvation.

Corrie ten Boom

(Quoted from the book entitled: Prison Letters, c. 1975 by Corrie ten Boom, Special Edition, published for Billy Graham Evangelistic Film Ministries, Inc., Published by Fleming H. Revell Company, p. 105)

Apart from the remarkable act of grace and forgiveness, what is most revealing to me about this letter was she wrote it on the same day she found out who her betrayer was. She was committed to following the example of Jesus who prayed on the cross "Father, forgive them, for they do not know what they do." (Luke 23:34)

Corrie went on to write a best-selling book, *The Hiding Place*, and a movie was produced with the same title. She was one of the heroines of the Resistance; and became one of the most remarkable evangelists in her later years until she passed away on her ninety-first birthday, April 15, 1983.

With the Global Outreach summer missions program in 1976, I had the privilege of visiting The Hiding Place in Haarlem (now a museum) and returned there a second time in December, 2017.

One of the members of the ministry team was a girl named Riska Bosshardt, who was a volunteer tour guide for The Hiding Place museum. After seeing one of the Psalm 91 scrolls I had brought on the trip, she told me that Corrie's father would often read Psalm 91 out loud during the war, and Corrie eventually memorized the whole chapter. Riska then asked if they could have one of the scrolls to hang in the building.

What she did not know was that I had been praying for an opportunity to leave a scroll in a public place; somewhere my little sister might see it and happen upon my contact information. For a couple of years, I had no idea where she was, but I thought it was possible that she and Dad could be in the Netherlands. It was 1976—if you lost contact with a family member, there was no Internet available to assist with a search—just intuition and prayer. My guess was that Dad had taken her to the Netherlands to avoid a custody battle, so hanging a scroll in the Hiding Place, with my name and contact information on it was an answer to a specific prayer.

The Psalm 91 scroll—displayed for a season in The Hiding Place—was a small gift from me. In return, I received peace of mind.

A couple of years later, I was able to locate my Dad and my sister. I sensed the answer to my prayers was in God's timing, which is always the right timing. The scroll was not needed for contact purposes in the Netherlands, I located my Dad and sister who were still in Canada, but in another province.

As you go through life, your siblings always have a special place in your thoughts and prayers, even if you did not get to grow up with them, or circumstances caused a wedge between you. I continue to pray for my family, for all of them to understand and receive the life-giving gospel message. It is only through Jesus that we can get to heaven.

Honestly, it is fun to share the scriptures. You never know where life's journey will take you. I never met Corrie in person, but I did receive a letter from her.[10] Nevertheless, I know I will have the pleasure of meeting Corrie in eternity.

Though she claimed public speaking was not one of her talents, Corrie used what abilities she had to reach as many people as she could. Corrie was never too busy with life to share the gospel. She lived in the present, taught lessons from the past, and informed almost everyone she met that they too can live for Jesus, and have hope for their future.

She didn't retire, she *re-fired*.

---

10 Letter included in the next section of pictures. It was written in English by her assistant.

"Bid voor de vrede van Jeruzalem"
                                Psalm 122 : 6

                                August 23, 1976

    Dear Henny,

    Thank you so muc h for the beautiful poster
    to hang up..When Terri told me about how
    nice it was and that it would be very nice
    for the hall we had rented to receive all the
    guests we could not handle right away in
    the Beje, I asked her if she could try to get
    one from you. I didn't know that you were in
    Holland, please come again to see the Beje
    when it is open. I'll include a folder. Maybe
    by the time you receive this letter, you'll be
    back in Canada.
    Anyway, I took the poster to a shop where they
    can make glass in front of it. I don't know
    where it will be hanging, in the Beje or in
    Corrie's private house, but I am sure it
    will be a blessing to the people.

    You know, the Lord is in control also in your
    family situation and the Lord will bring ameeting
    with your sister in His perfect time. Just
    trust Him and follow Him completely.

    Many greetings in our Lord and Savior, and thank
    you again for the beautiful poster.
    In Jesus the Victor, your

                            Riska Bosshardt,

        For: Corrie ten Boom

    Ten Boom Stichting
    Julianalaan 32
    Overveen. Holland.   Tel. 023 - 252370
                                          Postgiro 648138

"**I am so busy.**
How can I find time to pray?

Ask for forgiveness. Ask to be cleansed of the sin of having no time to pray. We must begin and end each day with prayer. It could be that Satan is pushing you into too much work so that you cannot take time to pray.

Lord, forgive us that we too often major in minors. Thank You that we may pray." — Corrie ten Boom (Each New Day, p.49, published by Fleming H. Revell Company, 1977)

"but we will give ourselves continually to prayer and to the ministry of the word."
— Acts 6:4 (N.K.J.V.)

Calligraphy by H. Vanderpyl
March 10, 2018

CHAPTER 4

REPURPOSING AN ELLERSLIE GRAIN ELEVATOR

YOU MIGHT BE CANADIAN IF:

- You know what a toque is.
- You know how to pronounce and spell "Saskatchewan."
- "Eh?" is a very important part of your vocabulary, and more polite than "Huh?"
- You think it is normal to have a grain elevator in your backyard.

Grain Elevators and Lighthouses

A typical elevator was thirty-two feet square and about seventy-five feet high. Their size made them visible from afar. Seeing one in the distance, you could assume it belonged to a village or town, which indicated that there would be food, shelter, and services.

Grain elevators were built alongside railways at eight-to-ten-mile intervals. They had to be within a reasonable distance to facilitate travel in one day from the family farm to an elevator and back, using a horse-drawn wagon.[11]

> Grain elevators, which have been variously referred to as prairie icons, prairie cathedrals, or prairie sentinels, are a visual symbol of western Canada. Numbering as many as 5,758 in 1933, elevators have dominated the prairie landscape for more than a century with every hamlet, village, and town boasting its row of them, a declaration of a community's economic viability and a region's agricultural strength.
>
> As the first step in a grain trading process that moves the grain from producer to worldwide markets, the grain elevator was a strictly utilitarian building, designed to receive, store, and ship grain in bulk. However, in 1923 French architect Le Corbusier hailed the elevator's stark simplicity and unadorned geometric shape as the ultimate example of form following function. In his book, Towards a New Architecture, he wrote, "grain elevators and factories, the magnificent first-fruits of the new age."
>
> —The Canadian Encyclopedia, article by Jane Ross, published online March 1, 2006, last edited April 24, 2015

---

11   Source: The Canadian Encyclopedia.

Yes, grain elevators were once an integral piece to the prairies. And the landscape, flat or rolling, would not have been the same without them. Displaying the town's namesake on the most prized, visible building was not only logical, but celebratory: the ultimate prairie symbol.

When those of Dutch background paint a picture of the Netherlands, they often include a windmill; people who grew up near the ocean include a lighthouse. Lighthouses and windmills are prominent structures that mark much more than land and house, and much more than light; they hold *home* in our hearts.

Lighthouses have historically been beacons: flashing lights for helping sailors find their way back to a safe port. They were designed to emit light from a system of lamps and lenses, to serve as a navigational aid to marine traffic. They are strategically located to mark hazardous coastlines, and thereby assist maritime pilots at sea. In the past, they were widely used, but in recent years, the number of operational lighthouses has declined substantially, due to the increasing use of alternative electronic navigational systems.

I have never lived in the Maritimes, but in 2012, I visited on vacation. I visited Pier 21 and, since I had already been there (as a baby) when my family immigrated to Canada, I was honoured to wear the *Alumni* sticker. Also on my bucket list—to go to Peggy's Cove and see the famous lighthouse.

It occurred to me: when you see a lighthouse like the one at Peggy's Cove on a bright sunny day, you think of it as being just another historical building. But if you are going through a dark, intense storm while on a ship, you look for the light shining from the lighthouse to help you navigate. Coastal lighthouses, like prairie grain elevators, are disappearing. Nevertheless, for a season, they were easily recognizable objects by which one knew his position—*Landmarks*.

Focusing on important scriptures, The Jesus Elevator was not only recognizable, but one such landmark that provided light, and pointed us to our future—our eternity.

The past is foundational to where we are at in the present. We live by faith, and faith is not past tense (that would be history), it is not future tense (that is hope), so it has to be present tense (we are living it now). Reading the word (the Bible) has faith right there.

We live in the present. If we are wise, we learn from the past; we read and listen to those who have experienced things in life similar to what we are facing. Sometimes we need the light of a lighthouse to guide us. We always need the light of the scriptures to guide us. If you know the way—like Corrie ten Boom did—light it for others.

Why Have a Jesus Elevator at the Entrance to Edmonton?

Edmonton was incorporated as a town in 1892 and became a city in 1904. It became the capital of Alberta when the province was formed a year later, in 1905. Before that, Fort Edmonton was established during the fur trade in the 18th century as a Hudson's Bay Company trading post because it is strategically situated on the main waterway of the western prairies, the North Saskatchewan River.

Its location is also roughly on the northern edge of the economic divide between the highly productive farmlands of central Alberta, and the vast, resource-rich northern Alberta, containing the oil sands—the largest deposits of oil in the world. The Trans-Canada Yellowhead Highway (Hwy. 16) passes through Edmonton east/west, and the Queen Elizabeth II Highway (Hwy. 2) connects to the south and north. The QE2 Highway connects to the Alaska Highway and is currently part of the Canamex Corridor.

"(In 1942)—The Alaska Highway was officially opened on November 2. The road from Edmonton to Fairbanks, Alaska, was built as a military supply route because of fears of a Japanese invasion of Alaska. The massive project was the largest of its kind, and had a tremendous impact on the growth of Edmonton and its role as 'Gateway to the North.'"

"(In 1947)—Likely the most influential event in Edmonton's history came on February 13, when Imperial Oil's Leduc #1 drilling site blew in. The city almost immediately became a boomtown, with a new oil-based economy that fuelled a period of massive growth and continues to help drive the city today."

(above quotes from the book: Edmonton City of Champions, edited by Jamie Wilson with Allyson Quince, published by City of Champions Inc., first edition 1999, page 198)

As mentioned, I lived in Edmonton from 1966 to 1975, and in Leduc from 1975 to 1977. In the '70s, when the entire province boomed and Edmonton experienced rapid growth, the title "Oil Capital of Canada" was commonly used. Another slogan (due to various accomplishments, including sports—Let's go Oilers!) was the "City of Champions."

"Gateway to the North" seems the most appropriate moniker at the south entrance to the city. Ellerslie Road is actually "zero avenue," correlating to the list of Edmonton's numbered avenues. Within a kilometer south of Ellerslie Road, is Gateway Park, which welcomes visitors at this entrance to the city.

EDMONTON

Gateway to the North

An Illustrated History by John F. Gilpin

The book entitled *Edmonton, Gateway to the North*, by John F. Gilpin, summarizes the significance of Edmonton as follows:

> *Edmonton as a fort, town, and city, has played a diverse role in the history of Canada. Initially it emerged as a result of the transcontinental search for furs that began in the early 18th century. The fur trade as the basis of its existence was replaced in the 19th and 20th centuries*

by the search for agricultural land, mineral resources, and national security. [...]

Overriding these aspects of Edmonton's history has been its consistent role as a boundary community, a role that has had anthropological, geographical, and historical dimensions. Edmonton stands between the boreal forest and the plains, the Cree and the Blackfoot, and the Canadian Northern Railway and the Canadian Pacific Railway. Edmonton, as a result, has been a focus for the clash of these northern and southern interests. Either by necessity during the fur trade era or by choice after 1881, Edmonton has embraced the north as its hinterland unlike any other community in Canada.

By coincidence or divine appointment, the Jesus Elevator was strategically located at Ellerslie corner, the entranceway to the City of Edmonton, *the Gateway to the North*: an important message at an important location during an important time.

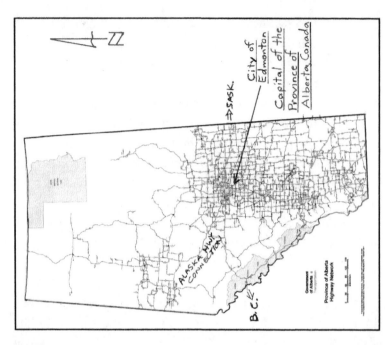

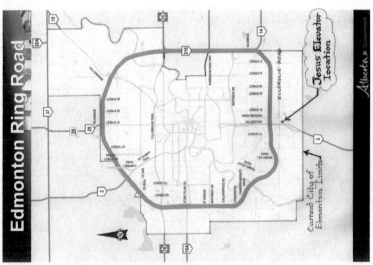

Location of the Jesus Elevator at the south entrance
to the City of Edmonton, Alberta, Canada

Other Alberta Wheat Pool Ellerslie Grain Elevator (demolished in 1995)

Former location of Jesus Elevator

Ellerslie Road

Jesus Elevator location (Hartley's Farm)

Highway 2 / Gateway Blvd.

Aerial Photo ~ circa 1988 ~

The Path is Marked by a Landmark

When I moved to Lethbridge in 1988, I worked on the University of Lethbridge expansion, which included the development of the first phase of a student housing complex and an interconnected pathway. At one of the planning meetings, the lead university engineer said a modern methodology for determining pedestrian pathway locations is to delay installation for one year and let the evidence of students' footprints decide their location. My boss, who had been raised in a South African boarding school, told us that with Africa's mountainous terrain, they would often release a herd of wild donkeys a couple years prior to road construction. Donkeys typically choose the path of least resistance, and once these paths are visible, you know where to build.

"But the question arises," my boss continued, "what do you do if you don't have donkeys? You hire engineers," to which the lead engineer responded, "It's a wise choice to use the word donkey instead of ass."

A path leads somewhere, and a landmark is a way-finding point.

I heard a sermon based on Andy Stanley's book: *The Principle of The Path—How to Get From Where You Are to Where You Want to Be*. Paths are mentioned often throughout the Bible.[12] The purpose of these paths, the pastor told us, is to get to a desired destination. There are, of course, decisions you can make that will take you on a different path.

I remember the moon-landing like it was yesterday. I was seventeen and fascinated. How does one even begin to plan a trip to the moon? Do you aim right at it, cross your fingers, and go? Had that been our strategy, mankind would still be trying to conquer this feat. Instead, NASA was not only intentional about where they were going, they performed careful calculations in choosing

---

12   Job 24:13; Psalm 23:3, 25:4, 119:105; Proverbs 3:5,6, 4:11, 4:26 and 5:21

the rocket's launch time and direction. They didn't want to get to where the moon might be or has been, they wanted to get to where it would be when they arrived. They wanted to land on it—to *get on it*.

It wasn't until I *got on it* by following the direction of Luke 15, and repenting from my sins, that I realized my pursuit of worldly gains would not profit me if my soul was not in right standing with the Lord Jesus (Mark 8:36). When we get to the end of our lives, we will not be judged according to our intentions.

I talked to a few people who remember the Jesus Elevator as a landmark indicator that they were arriving at the entrance to Edmonton. The landmark was a way-finding point that indicated they were getting close to home. In a parallel sense, the message on the elevator was pointing to our eternal destiny, our eternal home if we heed its message.

If you travel from Calgary to Edmonton, it is approximately three hundred kilometres—as the crow flies. If you used a compass (pretend this trip was in pioneer times) and your bearing was off by just one degree, you would miss your destination by about five kilometres. Not much if traveling by car, but a noticeable error if making the trip on foot.

When God took the Israelites out of Egypt, his intention was to bring them to the promised land, but the Israelites ignored His direction. The cost was so high, it was amortized over forty years… Seeing as one degree could cause a five-kilometre over-sight, and disobeying God could add as many as forty years to a trip, it's anyone's guess why we don't focus more of our time on choosing the right paths.

I attended a one-day Team Church Conference in Red Deer, Alberta on March 28th, 2019. During the lunch break, I met Larry Scheffelmaier and mentioned that I am writing a book about the Jesus Elevator. Larry did a lot of oilfield trucking over the years, and regularly passed by the Jesus Elevator. Without me prompting, here is what he had to say:

> *"It was always a wake-up call to read the verse on the Elevator. It was like God saying: 'you are on the wrong path, the wrong lane.' You probably have no idea how much good that verse did. I realized that it was God (speaking to me). Now I'm old and I understand that verse more. At 18 years old you still get the point, but as you get more knowledge it hits home more. It was a conviction, a reminder that 'I am going the wrong way.'"*

Larry described himself as a backslidden Christian but partially through the influence of God's word on the Jesus Elevator, he rededicated his life and accepted Jesus as Lord. (I received a text from him a couple days later giving me names of farmers who were neighbours to the Grain Elevator and could possibly give me some more inputs. In his text he said: "I pray a blessing on that book.")

In Proverbs 7:6-27, we are told a story of a young man who was tempted toward the path of impurity. It is all too easy to be snared by sin when you walk (run, leap, and dive) straight for it. We must pay attention to the things that capture our attention—for whatever captures one's attention (what you focus on) will also influence one's direction, and it is our direction—not our intention—that determines our destination. First comes life, then comes eternity. Focus on eternity.

CHAPTER 5

THE MESSAGE

Events Leading up to the
First Message on the Grain Elevator

Hartley Somerville was born on October 22, 1912 in southern Manitoba. Together with his brother Walter, they ran the family farm (livestock and grain operations) in southern Manitoba and expanded the family farm in the mid 1930s. The brothers were innovative in farm mechanization, replacing grain stooks and threshing machines with self-propelled combines.

> *The farmers who increased their holdings on perhaps the largest scale, in Manitoba, were Hartley and Walter Somerville. Their father, W.E. Somerville, came from London, Ontario, in 1889 with his father, who bought the east half of Section 6-6-22, five miles southeast of Hartney, Manitoba.*

[....] When flax for vegetable oil was in demand during World War II and its price reached $5.50 per bushel, Hartley and Walter sowed most of their acres to flax with such encouraging results that they decided, not only to seed all their farm with flax, but to buy or rent as many farms as were available and grow flax on them.

When training at the Souris and Hartney airports ceased, at the war's end, the Somerville brothers purchased the airport at Hartney from the War Assets Commission, to house the tractors, combines and other equipment necessary for their large-scale farming. Both Hartley and Walter secured pilot's licenses and bought a Tiger Moth airplane with which to supervise their widely scattered farms.

By 1947 they were operating thirteen sections of land, most of them in the Hartney district, but some as far away as Killarney and Crystal City. .... They bought a grain storage elevator of 30,000-bushel capacity at Argue siding, a mile from their home, and built another elevator of the same capacity at the farm itself. The men of their work crew, twenty-five to thirty-five in number, were housed at the airport and fed by the wives of two of the workmen. There Hartley maintained his headquarters while Walter and his wife lived at the home farm.

When their crops were sown in the spring of 1947, Hartley arranged that their combines and crews go south to Kansas, where the grain was ready for harvest earlier than in Manitoba, and do custom combining. The Somerville gang reached Kansas four days after leaving Hartney and for six weeks, working day and night shifts, they cut and threshed the Kansas wheat.

The men were housed in trailers and fed by women whose husbands worked on the gang. As the combines were often as much as sixty miles from one another in the Kansas fields, Hartley supervised the work by airplane. Working north from Kansas through Minnesota, the gang was back in Manitoba when the flax crop was ready for harvest.

That fall Hartley was married to Alice Dolmage and made a home in the officers' quarters at the airport.

In 1948 the Somerville brothers seeded over 4,000 acres of flax and 250 acres of Redman wheat and reaped a successful return.

As the price and return from flax decreased, the Somerville brothers reduced their acreage considerably and acquired road-making machinery with which to construct roads in both Manitoba and Saskatchewan. Over this work Hartley presides, while Walter oversees their still considerable farm acreage. Their enterprise has proven very successful and illustrates the possibilities that the new farm machinery opens to the aggressive Manitoba farmer.

Not many farmers in Manitoba equalled the Somervilles in the extent of their farm holdings, but there was an increase in the acreage of several farms, as their owners found that the cost of the new farm machinery was so high that it required the returns from a larger number of acres to meet the added expense of operation.

(Quoted from *The Mere Living, A Biography of the Hartney District* by Hazel McDonald Parkinson, 1957 p. 291-293)

An article appeared in the Ottawa Citizen newspaper on July 10, 1954 entitled "These Farmers Are Human Dynamos," continues the story.

(Uppper Photo: Walter Somerville (left) and brother Hartley in front of hangar at the airfield they bought. Lower Photo: Fleet of combines lines up on tarmac before proceeding to harvesting operations 15 miles away.)

Until recently, Hartley bridgehopped his Tiger Moth from field to field, delivering meals and instructions to harvesting crews, supervising the work of gangs operating the equipment with which they built a network of roads between farms—and also for other farmers and rural municipalities. Civil-aviation authorities frowned on such flying—"I reckon they didn't approve of such things as alighting on highways." Says brother Walter ironically—but by that time the roads were completed and now the Somervilles find it just as convenient to commute in their fleet of cars, trucks, and trailers.

The year 1948, in which they did not get much more than their seed back, was the year in which the brothers made up their minds that, while they would go the whole hog with mechanized farming, they would have no trust with scientific theories. "We had been going to seed half Royal flax and half Victory flax," says Hartley, "when the government Experimental Farm service came out with the statement the Royal flax would be good and Victory no good. So we took their advice and put in Royal, which yielded only four bushels to the acre, while Victory was giving 23."

Despite their prosperity the brothers—both of whom are married with families—live frugally. Walter, at the old home farm where the boys were brought up with Methodist strictness; Hartley, in a converted section of the former R.C.A.F. barracks building.

Unlike many farmers who relax out of season in the cities or in warm southern climates, theirs is a vacationless, year around job. With a crew of 10 to 15 men, they spend the winter overhauling their machinery. Last year they completed 10 miles of government highway between Hartney and Deloraine. [...] They are bidding on road contracts as they come up, including that section of the Trans-Canada Highway which will run near Brandon.

Why the brothers drive themselves so relentlessly is anyone's guess. Says Hartley, "I started out with the idea of being a millionaire by the time I was 50. We made money while the sun shone, but the sun isn't shining as brightly now. With the present cost of machinery and maintenance, and the way income tax keeps increasing, a man would be a fool to make any more. Reckon the only way we could be millionaires now is if they strike oil on our land."

The more easy-going Walter says briefly: "I hate to think we'll still be keeping up this pace when we're 60."

A relative who is not a farmer provided what is perhaps the best clue to the brother's driving force when he said: "The farm and district had been run down and abandoned for five years before Hartley and Walter took it over. Using modern methods, they cultivated it and made it pay handsomely. That sort of thing is their delight."

The brothers were innovative in farm mechanization, and they were named "the Flax Kings of Manitoba" by the Winnipeg Free Press. While Walter continued working on the Manitoba farm, Hartley moved to Alberta, raising his family on a farm in Ellerslie, Alberta, adjacent to the Highway 2 corridor at the entrance to Edmonton.

In 1964, Hartley purchased a nearby elevator and had it moved onto the farm. Shortly after, he had a discussion with local pastor, Mel Shareski. Mel wanted to erect a billboard with a gospel message along Highway 2—preferably near the entrance to Edmonton. The government refused his application but told him there were no restrictions for displaying messages on privately owned buildings. He discussed the idea with Hartley, who offered the use of his grain elevator. Around this time, the Alberta Wheat Pool sent men to remove their company name off the elevator, and Hartley and Mel saw it as a good opportunity to hire their services to paint the verse.

The following excerpt is from an article published in the Edmonton Journal on December 16th, 1976 p.31 (with corrected spelling of Hartley's last name):

> *Mr. Somerville feels divine guidance has helped him on several occasions during his 64 years. He talked of when he was 19 and how he used to ride a bale sling up and down from the ground to the hay loft.*
>
> *"I was in the loft one time and a voice said 'Hartley, let go,'" and the whole thing went right off the end of the carrier and fell to the ground. If I hadn't let go, I'd be dead right now." He said he looked around to see if his brother had spoken the words to him. He wasn't there and I knew God, Himself had spoken those words."*
>
> *That was a big turning point in Mr. Somerville's life. After that he began his search for the Lord in order "to know Christ." "I had a great load on my conscience in those days. I knew I was a sinner. By the time I was 22, I knew I had found Christ.*
>
> *"I knew that all I had to do was accept the fact I was a sinner. My sins were already paid for." The angels of heaven have been watching over him, said Mr. Somerville. On another occasion, a voice told him to look back at his wheel when he was about to take off in a small airplane.*
>
> *"I looked back and one tire was about nearly to blow out. But I was able to stop the plane."*

"He looks after me and the sign on the elevator is my opportunity to witness to the world what rings the bells in my heart."

Farmer painted message on grain elevator

(Source: Edmonton Journal, Dec. 16,1976 p.31)

In another news article published by The (Leduc) Representative, Nov. 26, 1975, Hartley explains some of the meaning behind the choice of the verse:

> *"There is joy in heaven over one sinner that repenteth,"*
> *Luke 15. [...]*
> *"Most people are pleased to see the words," said Mr.*
> *Somerville. "I know Jesus Christ saved my soul and I*
> *know he'll save others." [...]*
> *The quotation is a bit different from the book of*
> *Luke, chapter 15, verse seven. It reads "I say unto you,*

that likewise joy shall be in heaven over one sinner that repenteth..."

"*The sign shows the glorious relationship between life on earth and the angels in heaven," said Mr. Somerville. "It's self-evident."*

(Source: Somerville family photo.)

What was also self-evident was how big (both literally and spiritually) the message was. A grain elevator, measuring thirty-two feet wide and seventy-five feet high, if turned on its side, would be larger—much larger—than any standard billboard. For twenty-four years, until 1989, the elevator served as a prominent landmark, guiding the travellers who passed by.

I am not aware of another elevator or building that has displayed such a *big* message. This points to Hartley's character and his willingness to do something out of the ordinary to honour the Lord.

> *A man's heart plans his way, but the Lord directs his steps. —Proverbs 16:9*

The Jesus Elevator was the longest-running billboard scripture of its size during the years it stood, guarding the Gateway to the North.

The following excerpt came from the last paragraph of an article in the Western Catholic Reporter on September 20, 1982:

> *His main hopes with the sign are that he can encourage people to realize "there is more hope in this world than what is in this (immediate) world" and that it will encourage people to read the Bible.*

Through hard work, Hartley gained money, land, stature, and recognition among his peers. Nevertheless, his legacy wasn't the size of his farm and bank account, it was the life he weaved into his friends, family, and travellers—near and far—sharing the Word of God.

Events Leading up to the Second Message on the Grain Elevator

In 1978, through October 15-22, Canadian evangelist Terry Winter held a crusade in Red Deer, Alberta called *Parkland Alive*.

The event was held in the Capri Centre convention hall. It had wooden panelling above the podium area. "Now there's an ideal place to put a banner," I thought. I also painted a couple of street banners to hang on steel cables across the main street, Gaetz Avenue. This was a challenge because they were canvas banners and required flexible paint.

I was excited to tackle the one hundred-foot banner inside the convention hall, but when I measured it, I was disappointed to find it was only ninety-nine feet—a foot short. God, in good form, was kindly reminding me that the crusade was more important than my portfolio. In my prideful thinking, I wanted to be able to say that I did a one-hundred-foot banner. (Go big…or go home).

Mel Bowker directing the excellent Crusade Choir in the Capri Hotel Ballroom [notice the banner overhead. It ran the entire length of the ballroom and said, "Jesus said, I am the way, the truth and the life."]

Photo of part of the 99ft. banner. "Jesus Said: I Am The Way,
The Truth, and The Life." John 14:6
(Source: Terry Winter newsletter, Dec. 1978)

I used a two-and-a-half-foot wide newsprint roll and produced the ninety-nine-foot banner, written in my Olde English font: *"Jesus said: I Am The Way, The Truth, and The Life—John 14:6b"* This was the verse Terry Winter centred the crusade's message on. I decided to capitalize all of the words when I did the banner. The message was loud, powerful, and demanded the attention of everyone in the room.

In the audience was a young man named George Bradley. He told me afterwards that he was trying to listen to the message, but he kept glancing back and forth between the banner and the podium. Then, looking at the banner carefully, he realized: Jesus is The way, The truth, and The life. Right then and there, he knew he needed to follow Jesus with all priority and unashamed loyalty. That evening, at the altar call, he made a rededication to Jesus, his Lord and Saviour.

George worked as an employee of the Capri Centre, and he felt compelled to make a public confession of following Jesus. Up until this time, his testimony had been hidden and compromised by a spirit of timidity. This was the only night during the crusade that Terry Winter included in his invitation "perhaps you are here tonight and you are a born-again Christian, and God is calling you to come forward and acknowledge Christ publicly."

This night was pivotal in the Lord bringing George into relationship with spirit-filled charismatics who were going to lead him into a bolder spiritual walk.

George and I ended up attending the same church, and we became friends. He was also a student in one of the calligraphy classes I taught, and he picked up on the techniques almost as quickly as he absorbed spiritual truths. George became a pastor and currently ministers as the lead pastor for Liberty Christian Assembly in Red Deer.

Painting the Second Message on the Jesus Elevator

In the summer of 1979, one of my friends from Leduc called to see if I would be interested in re-doing the scripture on the Jesus

Elevator. Most of my friends drove past it on their daily trips into Edmonton, and they noticed that the message was fading, and especially difficult to read at night. One idea was to offer the farmer (Hartley Somerville) money to pay for a brighter spotlight. Meeting with Hartley and looking at the elevator up close, they realized the elevator siding was rotten in places and—in addition to a new spotlight—the whole building needed painting.

"Yes, I could do that," was my immediate reply. I had done big signs before (oversized posters, ninety-ninety-foot banner, etc.). To my surprise, they had already discussed the lettering style with Hartley, and he was good to proceed with Olde English lettering. With the task accepted, my mind began flooding with the logistics of painting an elevator. "How do they maintain the siding or do maintenance touch-up painting on grain elevators?" I asked.

"I suppose they dangle a guy on a rope…"

I wasn't overly fond of heights, nor had I ever scaled a wall in a harness. "I suppose I could dangle out there," I thought.

"Would you guys be able to measure the width and height of the elevator?" I asked. "And, the size of the current letters, please? If you can get me that, and a photograph of the current verse, I'll get to work."

It took me several hours to fall asleep that night. "How am I going to dangle from a rope, use a paint brush, and not drip bright, white paint onto the dark, red siding below?" I wondered.

Sometimes, talking is the simplest solution. When telling someone I was re-doing the scripture, they responded: "On plywood?"

"On plywood…?" I repeated. "But of course—on plywood! Why didn't I think of that?"

Doing it this way, I could cut each letter out individually and—with the painting already done on the ground—simply nail them into place. The wooden siding may have been weathered and beginning to rot, but with some longer nails, I'd be able to attach the letters to the solid wood behind it.

During the summer of 1960, I had watched my Dad use marine enamel to paint our family rowboat. Years later, between grades eleven and twelve, I worked on a painting crew with my stepdad; we not only painted houses, but we also did the woodwork staining, shellacking and varnishing. To top it off, my newly acquired father-in-law, who was also a professional painter, was a fountain of knowledge. Through these sources (and the endless, internal thoughts of an engineer), I knew the importance of getting a good undercoat of the *right* paint on new lumber.

Using the measurements and the photograph, I sketched the elevator to see how the new verse would fit. Once satisfied with the layout and corresponding dimensions, I went shopping.

"I need the best quality outdoor oil-based undercoat you have," I said to the paint sales representative. I wasn't concerned about the price. I wanted the new verse to stand the test of time—and in Alberta weather, no less. I purchased five gallons of undercoat and three gallons of gloss-white marine enamel, along with eleven sheets of quarter inch, good-one-side plywood and a four-inch paint brush.

I freehand painted the twenty-inch tall lowercase letters, then outlined the cutting edges with a pencil. It was a big job. And with the arrangements to repair the siding and repaint the elevator already underway, I was not yet dangling from a rope, but I was indisputably on the clock.

The Leduc fellowship, with the assistance of Hartley Somerville, hired the services of Steeplejack Scaffolding and painting contractor Allan Axelby to spray-paint the seventy-five-foot tall building. Also, to help us prepare the eighty-six pieces of plywood required for the verse, local chiropractor Don Pedersen was kind enough to let us use his woodworking shop.

If I had had more time, I might not have sought additional help. I didn't (thank God), so I enlisted help from my friend George Bradley, my nephew Richard Cote (who was visiting me that summer), Don Pedersen's son Bradley, and of course—Mary Anne. With saws buzzing a repetitive tune, we spent three evenings working late into the night, cutting out each piece—keeping Don Pederson up past his bedtime. (Thank goodness we weren't cutting out and painting all of Psalm 91!)

Before painting the letters—each with undercoat—we covered Don's driveway with weighed-down newspaper roll. We were careful to not only paint both sides of the letters, but the edges too, as we didn't want the wood to warp or rot when exposed to the elements.

The Christian in me was honoured to be doing such a prominent sign for Christ; the human in me was proud. Going very Big can lead to pride. Realizing this, I asked George to do one of the letters completely by himself. Letting go of the paintbrush can be difficult, but if Jesus, the only perfect person to ever walk the earth, chose imperfect people to do His work, I could at least trust my pal George with a letter. And yes, he had taken a few of my classes and was already familiar with my style, but sometimes we have to start with baby steps. And because we didn't have much time, I did the rest of the letters. The end result: I was just one of the painters, and I cannot claim to have done all the calligraphy for the Jesus elevator.

The installation of the letters was scheduled for the weekend of August 24-25, 1979. The scaffolding, which had already been set up for the repairs and repainting of the siding, was rented on a weekly basis and we did not want to incur the cost of an additional week. Realizing that we could not complete the painting of the letters before the scheduled weekend, we sent them—along with the paint—to a farm near Calmar: headquarters for the Agape

Force Ranch. The young men who lived and worked there were more than willing to help us finish painting.

At the elevator, we had two sets of swing scaffolds, which had steel cables supporting each end. We did not have an electrically powered hoist; it was all hand-cranking. One scaffold was ten feet long, to use for the narrow upper peak of the building, and the other was the full width of the elevator. I was told that the rigging worker from Steeplejack Scaffolding walked out onto the roof, sat down on the pointed peak, and—with his feet dangling over—had a smoke break. I'm not a smoker, but with a view like that, I bet it was the best smoke break of his life.

At ten feet, the scaffold was not wide enough, so fourteen-foot planks were nailed onto the platform. The modifications to the scaffold were done prior to me arriving on the site, so I did not have the benefit of seeing how well they were assembled. Engineering classes replayed in my head, and I was thinking about the cantilever effect. I thought about how you can use cantilever principles to pull nails out of planks, nevertheless, it was a scaffold, not a diving board. I was overthinking it, and if—for some reason—one of the cables were to fail, each of us was wearing a webbed-belt harness attached to a rope secured separately from the scaffold.

What a blessing it was to have George by my side.

We proceeded to ratchet our way to the top of the elevator. George, being a bit more athletic than me, was able to crank his end up faster which tilted the scaffold; but feeling like I might fall out was enough motivation for me to pick up the pace. Talk about a good workout.

Halfway up, I placed my hand on the wall siding, which swung the scaffold away from the wall, giving me an excellent view of the hundreds of rows of siding and the *little* people and *tiny* cars below. Instinctively, I once again reached for the wall, but that only pushed us and the scaffold further away. "George," I said, peeking over to see a concerned look in his eyes, "I just realized why it's called a *swing* scaffold."

As per my calligraphy font, the capital "J" for Jesus had two parts to it. We could not ratchet ourselves high enough to reach the top of the "J" while standing on the platform. "No problem," acrobat-George said before climbing onto the top of the scaffold rail. So that I could pass him the necessary piece when he was ready, I stood beside him. This meant we were both on the same end, and the scaffold was starting to tilt... but George didn't seem to mind.

All too casually, and on the tips of his toes, he nailed the top of the letter into place. Before long, the five-letter name—Jesus—was nailed to the elevator.

We then lowered the scaffold so it was just below the window and took a short break, climbing inside through the window and getting a ride down to ground level using the interior rope-operated elevator lift.

Our ground crew included a friend of mine, George Lamb, and my former typing teacher, Mr. Hank Kalke. Both George and Hank contributed to help cover the costs of the project. It was nice to be at ground level for awhile and view the word 'Jesus' at the top of the elevator.

During our break, we looked up to see Mr. Hank Kalke hanging out of the elevator window, wrapped in a white sheet and stretching out his arms in an *angelic* blessing-posture, waving theatrically toward Highway 2. He had a full beard and bore a striking resemblance to the typical artistic depiction of Jesus, and many vehicles were slowing down to take in the sight.[13]

We nailed the letters onto the wall using two-and-a-half-inch spiral shank nails, then, after finishing a line, we painted the nail-heads with marine enamel paint. Fortunately, I had brought some

---

13 Mr. Hank Kalke (coincidentally?) attended the Leduc fellowship, and had a good sense of humour.

of the scrap plywood, which turned out to be a huge blessing, as we needed several small pieces to fill in the space where the siding overlapped. You might know the saying: one man's scrap wood is another man's space-filler.

Things were going exactly as planned. At least they were until we descended upon the next word ("said")—just above the window. As we ratcheted the scaffold in place, dark clouds gathered, and the sky threatened to rain.

This caused concern because the letters needed one last coat of paint to cover up the nails. Knowing oil-based paint and rain don't mix well, George and I also knew it was time to pray.

As the sky grew darker, so did our fears…

At the end of that weekend of August 25th, 1979, we would all be returning to our regular day jobs. The thought of highway travellers being left in suspense for a full week, guessing what Jesus was trying to say was not only embarrassing, but one step below blasphemous in my mind. Plus, waiting till the next weekend would have doubled the cost of our scaffold rental, and in the process, bulldozed our budget.

Had we allowed ourselves to be directed by fear, we might never have made our deadline, but through prayer and hard work, we directed ourselves accordingly. We felt a few minor sprinkles during our morning coffee break, but we got back on the scaffold and the rain never bothered us again.

When you get on something for God, God gets on it, too.

The third line "what shall" (which was the first line requiring the full-width swing scaffold), proved to be another challenge. The scaffold switch went as planned, but since its cables were anchored through the elevator's side-windows, it continuously skidded along the sloped roof, providing a recurring sequence of surprise-recoils. This made for a bit of a scary ride.

I think George saw my knees knocking a bit, and did his best to encourage me. "It's like we're a couple of Air Canada pilots, Henry; we even have our own ground crew."

There were several people on the ground, helping us by tying the next set of letters onto one of the ropes hanging from the scaffold. We needed space to work on the platform, so we couldn't have all the letters at once.

When I was caught off-guard by another series of jerks, George said, "Just think, Henry, if the rapture happens while we're up here, we'll be there a split second before the rest of 'em!"

By the time we got to the fourth line, I was (fairly) relaxed and confident. George was right: we had our own ground crew; we had an advantage if the rapture happened; and we were making progress.

On the next few pages are photographs of the banners, followed by the scaffolding set-up and progress as we completed the second message on the Jesus Elevator. We had Kodak cameras in 1979, so some of the photos are black and white. Still, you can see the scary progression of the weather that day.

Portion of 99 ft. Banner and 40 ft. Street Banners.

Henry working on red outlines

One of the canvas street banners

*Assisted by volunteers Leonard and Kelly Beauchamp and Mary Anne Vanderpyl
(in the background)*

Chiropractor friend Don Pedersen was kind enough to lend us the Use of his garage and workshop. Of course, on our break, we tried out his Swimming pool.

Nephew Richard Cote, Henry Vanderpyl, George Bradley, Bradley Pedersen. – What could we spell with the letters that were already cut… but we did work hard. (notice Henry and George both had red knees)

Mary Anne Vanderpyl and Bradley Pedersen having fun with the Backwards letter "g"

Making progress .... painting the letters

George Bradley wearing the safety belt

On the scaffold are Henry (bluejean jacket) and George Bradley.
Hank Kalke (bluejean jacket) and unknown volunteer is assisting on the ground.
Notice the plank that was nailed to the bottom of the scaffold to extend
the Width on either side.

Notice that there are two separate parts to the letter "J"

On our way to higher heights while Henry tries unsuccessfully to Stop looking down.

Finishing the narrow scaffold work.

Now ratcheting the wide scaffold towards the sloped roof

Line four almost completed.

Completion Photos

The final descent. We had to push the swing scaffold out from the Wall to get past the grain discharge piping. The ground crew assisted with ropes.

Acrobat George re-hydrating. (we didn't have disposable water Bottles in 1979.)

Photo of cardboard models of the two messages--models made by the late Jim A. Pearson of 'Vanishing Sentinels

Photo of Alice Somerville and Henry Vanderpyl + cardboard models of the elevator.

The Effective Message of Scripture:

Hartley Somerville was in Manitoba the weekend we installed the verse. When he returned, he was pleasantly surprised to see the finished product.

The Edmonton Journal interviewed him on September 15th, 1979.

Hartley Somerville's "Jesus Elevator" has been given a facelift and a new spiritual message.

Since the mid-'60s, Mr. Somerville's red grain elevator close to Highway 2 has been reminding passers-by that "there is more joy in Heaven over one sinner that repenteth."

But it's not just joy that drops from heaven. Rain and snow had faded the scriptural message on which he and Alliance Church pastor Mel Shareski decided in 1965.

A group of young Christians from nearby Leduc turned up recently at the Somerville farm, asking if they could offer a stronger spotlight to give the elevator better lighting at night.

And, they hinted, they'd be more than willing to paint the building.

Mr. Somerville liked the idea–and decided it was also time to switch to another scriptural tack.

"We thought it was about time for a more striking, more provocative message."

Members of the Leduc group each put forward his choice. Mr Somerville prayed for guidance.

The result? Well, drive south and as you hit the Ellerslie turnoff, glance to your left.

There, by day or night, you'll read the words of the evangelist Mark, asking you what's the profit if you gain the world and lose your soul.

"Many people don't think they have a soul," says the Ellerslie farmer. "But human life is just 70 years long. Then eternity begins."

Spreading that news is the aim of his elevator messages, which have drawn hundreds of photographers from as far afield as Texas and England.

The familiar landmark has even worked its way on to mail addressed to his neighbors. One, who lives across from the elevator, still receives letters addressed to his house, "across from the Jesus Elevator."

District Journal

David Somerville and new message

'Jesus Elevator' gives motorists food for thought

DAVID MAY

ELLERSLIE — Harvey Somerville's "Jesus Elevator" has been given a facelift and a new spiritual message.

Since the mid-'60s, Mr. Somerville's red grain elevator close to Highway 2 has been reminding passers-by that "there is more joy in Heaven over one sinner that repenteth."

But it's not just joy that drops from heaven. Rain and snow had faded the scriptural message on which he and more had faded the scriptural message on which he and Alliance Church pastor Mel Morrow decided in 1965.

A group of young Christians from nearby Leduc turned up recently at the Somerville farm, asking if they could offer a stronger spotlight to give the elevator better lighting at night.

And, they hinted, they'd be more than willing to paint the building.

Mr. Somerville liked the idea — and decided it was also time to switch to another scriptural tack.

"We thought it was about time for a more striking, more provocative message."

Members of the Leduc group each put forward his choice. Mr. Somerville prayed for guidance.

The result? Well, drive south until as you hit the Ellerslie turnoff, glance to your left.

There, by day or night, you'll read the words of the evangelist Mark, asking you what's the profit if you gain the world and lose your soul.

"Many people don't think they have a soul," says the Ellerslie farmer. "But human life is just 70 years long. Then eternity begins."

Spreading that news is the aim of his elevator messages, which have drawn hundreds of photographers from as far afield as Texas and England.

The familiar landmark has even worked its way on to mail addressed to his neighbors. One, who lives across from the elevator, still receives letters addressed to his house, "across from the Jesus Elevator."

Source: Edmonton Journal news article, Sept. 15,1979 p.H12

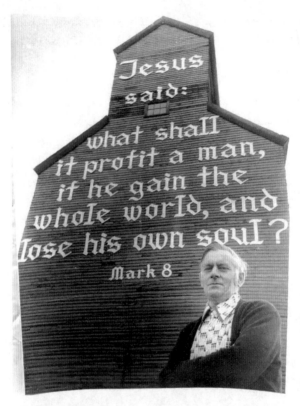

Source: Edmonton Journal news article, Sept.15,1979 p. H12,
photo of Hartley Somerville.

If Canada Post had no difficulty understanding these directions, then you know that it was a prominent and well-known landmark.

At a prayer meeting in 1975, a girl shared her testimony, which involved running away from home. Traveling south, she saw the Jesus Elevator (with the old verse) while exiting Edmonton. As she read and reread Luke 15, she began questioning the path she was on. "Is this the direction God wants for my life?" she asked herself. Pulling onto the shoulder, she realized: as big as her problems might be, *God was bigger.* Without another thought, she turned around, returned home, and—with God—made it through her circumstances.

In August 2013, a man by the name of Frank Remley shared his testimony with me regarding the events leading up to an *eventful* day on October 4, 1981:

> *When I was fourteen, I lived in Thorhild, and regularly travelled to Red Deer to help in the family stucco business. I grew up in a Christian home and knew about Jesus, but did not know Him as my personal Saviour. I was a spiritual prodigal, running away from the Lord. But every time I drove to Red Deer, I glanced at the Jesus Elevator, even though I didn't always want to.*
>
> *In 1979, the verse was switched from Luke 15 to Mark 8. I knew both verses. In 1981, I flew to Calgary to see my sister. The Holy Spirit was after me and was convicting me that entire weekend. On my way to the airport, I saw the scripture and it was deep in my thoughts. God was speaking to me. I got onto the airplane and there was a guy across the aisle, a Bible open on his lap the entire flight. For the next three quarters of an hour, I thought about those verses while watching this guy.*
>
> *During that weekend, I stopped at a restaurant in Calgary where I was confronted with a bookstand full of Christian books. I flew back to the Edmonton International Airport. I had planned to drive home, but heading north on Highway 2, was feeling conflicted. I also knew I would have to see that elevator again. I finally broke down and—right there on the shoulder of the highway—I stopped the car, prayed and accepted Jesus as my Lord and Saviour.*

Though Frank knew both verses on the Jesus Elevator, he had been running away from the eternal inheritance God was offering him. "But after I got saved," he stated, "the verse never bothered me again. I really missed it when it was torn down."

Thoughts Regarding Luke 15:7 and Mark 8:36

Our souls are more valuable than the world and everything that is in the world.

> *Why should I fear when evil days come, when wicked deceivers surround me—those who trust in their wealth and boast of their great riches? No one can redeem the life of another or give to God a ransom for them—the ransom for a life is costly, no payment is ever enough—so that they should live on forever and not see decay. For all can see that the wise die, that the foolish and the senseless also perish, leaving their wealth to others. Their tombs will remain their houses forever, their dwellings for endless generations, though they had named lands after themselves. People, despite their wealth, do not endure; they are like the beasts that perish. —Psalm 49:5-12 (NIV)*

And, the scripture from Luke 15 states:

> *I say unto you, that likewise joy shall be in heaven over one sinner that repenteth, more than over ninety and nine just persons, which need no repentance. —Luke 15:7 (KJV)*

Luke 15 contains three parables. In the first, a shepherd leaves behind ninety-nine sheep to find one that went missing. When he finds it, he and his friends rejoice. The second is about a lost coin. When the owner finds it, she and her friends rejoice. The third is about a father who, upon his prodigal son's return, accepts him with open arms and gathers his servants to rejoice.

Before accepting Jesus, I also was reading Luke 15, but it wasn't until I accepted Him that these parables started to make sense. No matter our situation, background, net worth—or friend-count on social media—we have everything to gain by *running home to God.*

> *What good will it be for someone to gain the whole world, yet forfeit their soul? Or what can anyone give in exchange for their soul? —Matthew 16:26 (NIV)*

The entire world is worth less than one soul.
But God demonstrates His own love toward us, in that while we were still sinners, Christ died for us. —Romans 5:8

> *For I delivered to you first of all that which I also received: that Christ died for our sins according to the Scriptures, —1 Corinthians 15:3a*

The second Jesus Elevator verse (from the book of Mark) is repeated in the book of Luke. *Profit* is also referred to in the book of 1 Timothy.

> *For what shall it profit a man, if he shall gain the whole world, and lose his own soul? —Mark 8:36 (KJV)*

> *For what is a man advantaged, if he gain the whole world, and lose himself, or be cast away? —Luke 9:25 (KJV)*

*But reject profane and old wives' fables, and exercise
yourself toward godliness. For bodily exercise profits a
little, but godliness is profitable for all things, having
promise of the life that now is and of that which is to
come. This is a faithful saying and worthy of all accep-
tance. —1 Timothy 4:7,8,9*

Regarding the above verses, it is apparent: both messages on
the Jesus Elevator were pulling us toward the heart of the gospel.
Signs—steering passersby toward the right path, the right direction—not in a literal sense of course, but in life.

In choosing the path to repentance, we also need to seek the
things from above—Godly things—like the will of the Lord, and
in turn—His love.

Thou Shalt ~~Not~~ Make Mistakes

I do not profess to be perfect. This was evident when we got to the
fifth line on the Jesus Elevator. The King James Version says, "if he
shall gain the" so the verse should have read:

Jesus
said:
what shall
it profit a man,
if he shall gain the
whole world and
lose his own soul?[14]

---

14   In the NKJV, the verse reads: "What will it profit a man if he gains the whole
world, and loses his own soul?"

We cut out two sets of letters for the word "shall" but by that time, the mistake was already made. On my planning sheet, I had not included the width of the second "shall," as it was already calculated in a previous line. And with the first four lines already nailed into place, the only way we were going to fit in the second "shall" was by cutting new, smaller letters or by adding an eighth line to the verse. For solutions, they seemed worse than the problem, so I opted to delete it.

Full disclosure: at the time of writing, I still have the tracings for the second "shall" in storage—a combination, perhaps, of *unredeemed* pride and *overly-redeemed* regret. Pride says, "I never make mistakes. I thought I did once... but I was wrong." Regret says, "Everything happens for a reason. But sometimes the reason is because I made a bad decision."

After we completed the second verse, I should have been smiling ear to ear. We didn't know exactly how long the project should have taken, but we were sure we had done it in record time.

Regret can and will steal your joy.

After admitting that I was struggling to accept the error, my crew unanimously agreed: the intent of the message was unchanged. Later on, I also realized that the original Luke 15 verse was not a word-for-word copy either, yet its meaning was still adequately conveyed. This made me feel better.

Isn't it odd how we sometimes need to see others make the same *mistake* before we can forgive ourselves?

Calligraphy and engineering developed in me a quest for perfection. Yet, it is not perfection that has given me the ability to teach others—it's my mistakes, my trials, my errors. It is the times I have fallen, and gotten back up—the times I have felt like quitting, yet have continued to fight the good fight that provide the best lessons.

When I was asked in 1979 to paint the second scripture, it fit my motto: "*Go Big or Go Home,*" so I did not hesitate. Though I had never scaled a building before, I had acquired a good deal of experience with larger signs. I was the man for the job. The Leduc fellowship knew it. I knew it. And most importantly, God knew it.

The Lord prepares us for a task before assigning it. We just have to be willing to follow, through trial and error—and sometimes, to the end of our rope—His leading.

> And we know that all things work together for good to those who love God, to those who are the called according to His purpose. —Romans 8:28

Spiritual Opposition Towards the Landmark Message

The Jesus Elevator had a monumental feel to it during its twenty-four years in ministry. Like the lighthouse that lights the way home for sea-travellers caught in a storm, the Jesus Elevator provided *spiritual light* for those caught in the storms of everyday life.

To believe in the Bible is to believe in the spiritual side of life—and with it, the spiritual warfare taking place all around us:

> For we do not wrestle against flesh and blood, but against principalities, against powers, against the rulers of the darkness of this age, against spiritual hosts of wickedness in the heavenly places. –Ephesians 6:12

This is evident with the proliferation of Satan-worshipping cults.

There was a news article in the Edmonton Journal dated January 31, 1984, about a murder that occurred in May of '83—not far from the Jesus Elevator. The article tells of a twenty-seven-year-old man who strangled and killed a sixteen-year-old boy, whose first name was Mark.

The article quotes the killer:

> I had to kill somebody called Mark, as he represented the frustration that I couldn't answer the question on the sign." In the court statement of facts, the killer "told police that he was controlled by outside forces, and someone was telling him he was the devil when he killed the youth."
>
> A forensic psychiatrist testified at the trial that the killer "[...] would send notes to people selected randomly from the telephone book [...] He (the killer) said that the whole world was after him, so he hid in a ravine, waiting for the people to whom he had sent notes to rescue him in a spaceship.

To say the message on the Jesus Elevator, and specifically the reference to "Mark," was what drove this man to kill someone by the same name is—well … *insane*. Compare it to an "Oh Henry" billboard campaign promoting their peanut-caramel-fudgy chocolate-coated candy bars. Would someone, not understanding how the combination of these four ingredients could be so incredibly delicious, feel the need to kill a Henry—like me…? I certainly hope not.

Obviously, the killer had serious issues with his mental health. He was found to be not guilty of second degree murder by reason of insanity.

God's Word is powerful, the thief (Satan) knows it and will do everything and anything to distort it.

> The thief does not come except to steal, and to kill, and to destroy. I have come that they may have life, and that they may have it more abundantly. —John 10:10

Just as Corrie ten Boom recited Psalm 91 in the Hiding Place, we too can shine light upon our own trials and tribulations whenever we dive into God's Word. Years later, when meeting the Nazi guard who murdered her sister, Corrie was faced with the difficulty of forgiving a fellow human being and making sense of a senseless crime. By doing so, she was able to shine the goodness of God, not only on this undeserving man, but demonstrate—on a large scale—an example of true (and difficult) forgiveness.

The killer says it was the elevator's message that led him to murder, but in reality (in spirit and in truth), we know it was not. He dwelled on the satanic influences and ended up killing an innocent 16 year old; but there is still hope for him if he repents. People under demonic oppression can be delivered and set free by the Word of God. Satan fears the unadulterated proclamation of scripture; for this reason, he will always distort and attach lies whenever quoting it.

When God brings conviction of our sins, we can try to hide it or we can confess and repent. In the Old Testament, we learn that King David sinned—and sinned *big*. He committed adultery and murder, then tried (in vain) to cover it up. The Biblical principle of sins coming to light becomes evident when he is confronted by the prophet Nathan.[15]

King David's heart broke when he came face to face with his sin; he expressed that brokenness in Psalm 51, where he cries out to the Lord for a new nature. He (genuinely) wanted to be different, and in the tenth verse, pleads:

> *Create in me a clean heart, O God, and renew a stead-fast spirit within me. Do not cast me away from Your presence, and do not take Your Holy Spirit from me.*
> *—Psalm 51:10*

---

15   See 2 Samuel 12:1-12

King David understood our deepest human need—to have a transformed heart. It is not enough for us to simply become a better person; we need to be renewed. The Holy Spirit is able and willing to do that. He will give you a new spirit—the Holy Spirit—to fill and empower you, and with your participation, will recreate in you a pure and Godly heart.

Whenever you need a compass recalibration—or a full life-transformation—correction is but a (repent-ful) step away. Pray the prayer King David did in Psalm 51. The sin might be big, but our God is bigger, and you, my friend, are saved by God's never-ending grace.

> *But where sin abounded, grace abounded much more,*
> *so that as sin reigned in death, even so grace might*
> *reign through righteousness to eternal life through Jesus*
> *Christ our Lord. –Romans 5:20b-21*

The Demolition of the "Jesus Elevator"

In 1981, Hartley and Alice Somerville made plans to move to another farm near Airdrie, Alberta, and they put their Ellerslie property up for sale. Life events include changes, and there is no guarantee that things will stay the same. The property was sold, but there was some discussion with the buyer of the property that the Elevator was to be kept there as a south Edmonton landmark.

On the morning of December 2, 1989, the elevator was bulldozed. Hartley's son and daughter-in-law were notified by someone who happened to go by the site that morning and saw the demolition in progress.

The original buyer, Daon Developments, was bought out by BCE Development corporation (a Calgary subsidiary of Canadian telecommunications giant, Bell Canada). There was a demolition permit issued by the Edmonton planning department. An Edmonton Journal article, dated December 2, 1989, included a photo showing the elevator's ruins.

Obviously, there were strong feelings and reactions on the part of the Somerville family. They were given no notice that the demolition would take place; if notice had been given, perhaps there would have been a different end result. The demolition was done quickly, and afterward, in cleaning up the mess, there was also some blatant disregard of the burning permit's conditions, and the smoke caused traffic hazards and windblown embers risking the spread of fire. The land remained vacant for a few years after the demolition, and then it was developed into a commercial subdivision.

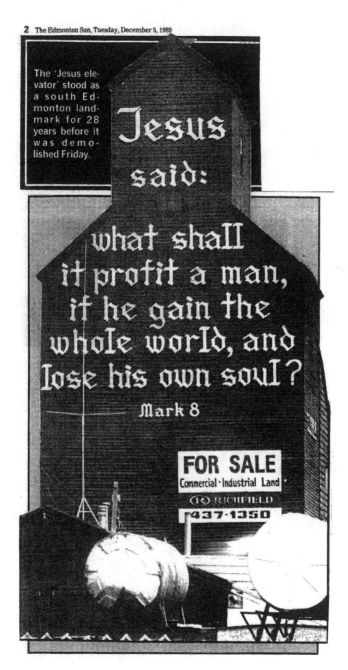

2 The Edmonton Sun, Tuesday, December 5, 1989

The 'Jesus elevator' stood as a south Edmonton landmark for 28 years before it was demolished Friday.

Jesus said:

what shall it profit a man, if he gain the whole world, and lose his own soul?
— Mark 8

FOR SALE
Commercial · Industrial Land
RICHFIELD
437-1350

Source: The Edmonton Sun, news article Dec. 5, 1989 p.2

Saturday Dec. 2, 1989
The Edmonton Journal

Lynn Somerville and husband John — son of former owner Hartley — survey the elevator's ruins   Brian Gavriloff The Journal

Bulldozer fells landmark 'Jesus elevator'

Source: Edmonton Journal news article Dec. 2, 1989 p.61

Millions of Views Per Year

Though the Jesus Elevator was demolished, the Message of the scriptures will never pass away—nor will their impact be lost.

> *Heaven and earth will pass away, but My words will by no means pass away. —Matthew 24:35 (see also Mark 13:31)*

> *For the things which are seen are temporary, but the things which are not seen are eternal. —2 Corinthians 4:18b*

In April of 2018, it was reported that two Toronto highway digital billboards are considered to be Canada's current largest billboards:

> *Astral, Bell Media's out-of-home (OOH) advertising business, has unveiled what are reportedly Canada's largest highway digital billboards. The two 17 x 8.5m (56 x 28-ft) faces stand beside Toronto's Gardiner Expressway, near Exhibition Place.*
>
> *Both structures were converted from static billboards to digital screens. Their highway locations deliver an average of 116,000 daily impressions.*

(Source: www.SignMedia.ca , news topic dated April 30,2018 accessed May 13,2020)

Though it might never be formally classified as a billboard, I think it is accurate to state that, from 1965 to 1989, the Jesus Elevator was the largest scripture sign displayed in the country. The size of the Jesus Elevator was significant, but I did not realize how significant it was until I began researching for this book.

The elevator was strategically located just north of the Edmonton International Airport, at the south side entrance into Edmonton. Based on the Average Annual Daily Traffic (AADT) numbers from the Alberta Transportation website, there were millions of people who viewed the two scripture messages during the twenty-four years it existed. Using the AADT traffic counts, the number of views per year can be calculated as follows:

YEAR	AADT (Combined Northbound & Southbound)	MILLIONS OF VIEWS PER YEAR	AVERAGE	TOTAL VIEWS
First Message				
1965	8,575 views x 365 days	3.13 M		
			4.08 M x 6 yrs	24.5 M
1971	13,770 views x 365 days	5.03 M		
			7.41 M x 8 yrs	59.3 M
Second Message				
1979	26,840 views x 365 days	9.80 M		
			11.57 M x 10yrs	115.7 M
1989	36,560 views x 365 days	13.34 M		
	Less Dec. 2-31			- 1.1 M
		TOTALS	24 yrs	198.4M

There were over three million views per year in 1965, increasing to just under ten million views in 1979 and thirteen million views in 1989. Averaging the numbers, the first message had approximately eighty-four million views in fourteen years and the second message had approximately one hundred fourteen million views in ten years.

That is a total of approximately one hundred ninety-eight million views of life-changing scripture.

Hartley did things in a big way, so God provided him with a calligrapher who also did things in a big way. Nevertheless, we both recognized we serve a much bigger, infinite God, and that without Him, our ways are not only small, but meaningless.

Go big or go home. Or, as I could imagine Hartley saying: Go big, but not for yourself. Go big for God. And when your time is done, He will bring you home.

To display such a large sign and receive millions of views is remarkable. It could be argued that some of the vehicles passing the elevator were occupied by people who did daily commutes. It would be hard to determine how many different people viewed the message. Many of the vehicles would have more than one passenger. Also, with the proximity of the Edmonton International Airport, many airline passengers viewed the Jesus Elevator during take-off and landing. Whatever the number, it is obvious that it was well-viewed. The number is big, which is part of the legacy.

CHAPTER 6

LEGACY... IT'S NOT ABOUT YOU

Wayne Gretzky is indisputably a Canadian hockey legend. There are numerous videos documenting his remarkable accomplishments. One very notable video is a 57-minute documentary titled "Above and Beyond". It documents his career starting when he was a 3-year-old growing up on the family farm in Brantford Ontario and he just loved to ice skate on their outdoor rink.

At about the 10-minute mark of the video, Wayne Gretzky's move to the City of Edmonton to play for the Edmonton Oilers is introduced with an aerial view of the farmland approaching the south entrance to the City. It then focuses on the Jesus Elevator pausing long enough so you can read the message: "Jesus said: What shall it profit a man, if he gain the whole world, and lose his own soul?—Mark 8". As the narrator states:

"If pro football had its Green Bay, then pro hockey was to have its Edmonton. This golden farmland would become the unlikely backdrop for one of hockey's most impossible dynasties. Mature beyond his years, the adored young millionaire Gretzky would lead this historic charge with the values he was taught on the farm.

Not yet 18 years old, Wayne Gretzky again proved the skeptics wrong. Number 99 made the W.H.A. (World Hockey Association) all-star team and realized the dream of playing with his boyhood hero Gordie Howe."

Wayne Gretzky played in the N.H.L (National Hockey League) for the Edmonton Oilers and lead them to win the Stanley Cup four times. At about the 27-minute mark, the narrator states:

"But Gretzky, the scoring machine and hockey ambassador, was a different breed. The farther his talents took him, the more he thought about where it had all begun."

Wayne Gretzky then states:

"You know we talked about how my Dad made me a hockey player, about how my Dad put me in the N.H.L., you know the sacrifices that my mother made, not going out on Friday night because you know we need the money to buy a new pair of skates or not buying new curtains because I needed new hockey sticks, you know things like that a lot of parents just don't do."

In 1988, Wayne was traded to the Los Angeles Kings hockey team. Bruce McNall, the King's Owner found out about Wayne's character early on. Wayne told him during the wage negotiations that *"if you want to pay me that much, why don't you take a certain portion of it and divide it among all my teammates as a bonus."* Bruce McNall stated that it was a business deal he will always remember.

Gretzky's passes turned average players into good ones and good players into great ones. As one of his teammates, Marty McSorley, stated: *"You get caught up in his attitude, his skill, and his confidence. It's a lift for everybody. He never says anything negative."*

Wayne Gretzky broke the all-time leading scorer record that Gordie Howe held after 26 years of playing hockey, but Gretzky did it in only 10 years. At about the 52-minute mark, the narrator states:

> *"He has averaged 180 points per season for 10 years, an unthinkable feat, a smashing of any standard set by any player with any scoring, and the grace with which he accepted these triumphs is a statement of his character."*

Obviously, Wayne Gretzky is a hockey legend and has a significant legacy, but is his legacy just the trophies and accomplishments, or is it his attitude in how he achieved those accomplishments as a team player?

Hartley Somerville had several accomplishments in the area of agriculture and contracting, but he also had a background attitude of wanting to serve others and help them along on the path of life. Life that ends in eternity.

There is a myriad of thoughts about what a legacy is all about. In my own career, I had thoughts of creating a legacy to have a street named after me.

I was employed with a consulting engineering company in the city of Red Deer, Alberta from 1977 to 1984 and helped design several new subdivision roadways. During those years, I worked with a professional planner, Mr. Dave Plumtree, who once told me a story about the Westpark Subdivision.

Since the plan called for street names starting with the letter "W,"—Mr. W.C. Wong—a successful businessman and one of the city's pioneers—was given the honour of having a street named after him. Coincidentally, one of the planners at the Parkland Regional Planning Commission was Mr. Frank Wong.

The initial plan, including the suggested street names, was circulated internally. One of the planners assigned the street names on the preliminary plan, naming a street as "Wong Way". Everyone, including Frank, had a good laugh. Seeing the confusion this could cause, they came up with the idea to instead name a short, one-block-long road with only side-yards, Wong Avenue. The end result is that no one had an address on Wong Avenue. This at least prevented anyone from having to re-enact an Abbott and Costello skit when giving directions to their house.

If you look at a Red Deer map today, in line with Wong Avenue but a bit further south is Wright Avenue, with about thirty-five residences having addresses on this avenue. Nevertheless, it didn't really matter, Wright or Wong, what mattered was they found a solution.

From 1998 to 2006, I worked on the engineering design of a large mobile home park named Station Grounds. The street names for the first couple of phases followed a railway theme that included Railway Street, Spurline Avenue, Yardmaster Avenue, Conductor Boulevard, and Porter Street. "After all these years working for you," I said to the developer, "maybe there should be some recognition in the next phase. What about Engineer Avenue?"

Believe it or not, he decided to incorporate Engineer Avenue into the next phase. Ask and you shall receive.

One thing I didn't ask for, however, was a difficult-to-spell last name. In my early days of engineering, a friend from work told me he kept an "idiot file" in which he saved the envelopes showing the various misspellings of his last name. "Now there's an idea," I thought, and immediately started my own file.

Over the years, I have (so far) collected forty-eight unique misspellings of my last name. Here are a few top contenders:

- *Vanderpipe* (good engineer name)
- *Vander Pile* (another good engineer name), at least the pronunciation is correct
- *Vander Pill* (yes, it was written on a prescription)
- *Vanderpepe* (no comment)

Incidentally, I once went to an office and a secretary asked me to spell my last name. I spelled out Vanderpyl and I noticed she added an "e" at the end. I told her, "There is no 'e' at the end," to which she replied, "Yes there is," to which I replied, "I know how to spell my own name."

Her face lit up like a bottle of ketchup.

Yes, I think—for now—I'll pass on having a street with my actual name on it. Engineer Avenue is good enough.

Often we assume legacy means having our name on a monument, building, facility or street sign, or that one is obtained through extra-generous, philanthropic giving. Names on bridges, monuments and scholarships may sound cool, and please the world (and our egos), but they are not everlasting.

A legacy is much more.

Like the spelling of our name, we are also the only ones who can (confidently) write the story that (hopefully) becomes our legacy. Some people will tell us what our legacy is or, with a little work, could be; but ultimately, it is up to us—and of course, the grace of God—to determine what is left behind when our time is finished.

I saw a sign posted on a wall in a senior's home that made me contemplate what the meaning of "legacy" is:

> *What you leave behind is not what is engraved in stone monuments, but what is woven into the lives of others. —Pericles*

While this definition is better than most, I would define legacy as "the everlasting evidence of a life lived glorifying Jesus Christ." What you weave into the lives of other people lasts an eternity, and also fulfills the Great Commission.

The Legacy of Hartley B. Somerville

> *The wise shall inherit glory, but shame shall be the legacy of fools. –Proverbs 3:35*

I never did meet Hartley Somerville.

Once tasked with *re-scripting* the Jesus Elevator, my focus did not waver from the planning and execution of the new verse. And, since Hartley Somerville was away the weekend we installed it, I missed my golden opportunity for getting to know the man behind Canada's biggest and longest-running billboard scripture.

Later, whenever I drove past the elevator, life seemed to always provide a reason for not pulling into the Somerville driveway and I figured Hartley was—more likely than not—also too busy. After all, farmers don't get paid by how many conversations they have in a day. For these same reasons, I also failed to pick up a phone and call.

Sometimes we learn the hard way. And though it doesn't feel good, the regret I have over never meeting or speaking with Hartley taught me an invaluable lesson:

You don't *find* time—you *make* it.

After he passed away, I researched his background and interviewed people who knew him best, including his family. Wherever I looked and whoever I talked to, one thing became obvious—Hartley was a follower of Jesus Christ, reading the Religion section of the newspaper before attending as many as four evangelical church services in a single Sunday. Instead of talking to people about his problems, he shared the gospel with them. This included neighbours, friends, family, and people driving onto his driveway to get a better view of the elevator—anyone and everyone. I believe his motivation was partially revealed in the Somerville quote: "Talking to people about their soul and eternal heaven is a pleasure to me."

Hartley was not just diligent in praying and sharing the gospel, he was also a hard worker—determined in everything he set his mind to. So much so that he and his brother were called the "Human Dynamos," which was an impressive nickname, considering the "Energizer Bunny" had not been invented yet.

Talking to Hartley's family, I asked what he was like during everyday family times:

> *"Dad said a prayer before every meal and would often end it by thumping his hand on the table, saying: 'Praise God! Maybe today we get to go to heaven.' Also, when he was heading out the door, if you asked him where he was going, he would usually say, 'I'm going to heaven.' He looked forward every day to being in heaven with Jesus."*

I also asked Hartley's wife, Alice, what it was like when Hartley died. She said it was hard, but not all that hard in the sense that she knew—beyond a doubt—that he was prepared to go to heaven.

For years he told his friends and family where he was going; this made it easier for Alice and others to accept his death.

Like an artist who paints a mural upon the work of an architect, I got to use my calligraphy gift by installing God's message upon Hartley's repurposed grain elevator. In life, there is a natural sharing of legacy. The Jesus Elevator is inherently more Hartley Somerville's legacy than mine; but Hartley, I'm sure, would quickly point out that, human hands aside, credit goes to our Lord and Saviour, Jesus Christ.

By human standards, Hartley was not famous. If any streets were named after him, I have not been on them. And, though his gravestone has the Jesus Elevator with the first verse etched into it, and the second Mark 8 verse engraved along the bottom, I have not come across a monument bearing his name and accomplishments.

Nevertheless, I could only imagine how they announced his arrival in Heaven...

> *Ladies and gentlemen, welcome to the main event. In God's corner, undefeated through the blood of Christ, standing tall with nearly two hundred million lives changed, he was a King of Flax, the other Human Dynamo Bro, the farmer, the preacher, the never-ending teacher... Give it up for God's one and only: HAAAARTLEEEEY SOMMMERVILLLLLLE!*

I can only imagine the standing ovation that followed.

Hartley did not shy away from telling people they must be born again (John 3:3-16), that "there is Joy in Heaven over one sinner that repenteth" (Luke 15: 7,10 KJV), and that earthly riches don't profit in eternity (Mark 8:36). People who knew him said he was consistently focused on Jesus.

Knowing the message inside his Bible was the only thing that would last forever, Hartley was steadfast in weaving the Word of

God and its message of love, joy, and freedom into the lives of those around him. He wasn't afraid to display scripture or share his heart—instead, he opted to be a walking, talking billboard for Jesus.

God's Word is worth sharing. In spreading the Good News and by praying for others, we not only improve life on earth, but direct ourselves toward the Gates of Eternity.

Hartley knew where he was going and he knew that God, through Jesus, made a way to get him there, and so he directed his life accordingly.

Some call it destiny. Others call it hope. But the true legacy of a man or woman isn't written in the stars… it is written in Heaven.

Gravestone Legacy Messages

My wife, Mary Anne, passed away from pneumonia-induced heart failure in January 2017. It was unexpected, traumatic, and irreversibly real. I performed CPR on the side of the road, then she was unresponsive in the intensive care unit for a day and half before passing away. We were three months away from our fortieth wedding anniversary.

About three years earlier, we had purchased family plots at the Horn Hill Cemetery, near Penhold, Alberta, where my wife's parents are buried. I wanted her gravestone to match the size and shape of her parents', so I called the monument company who manufactured them, aptly named: Legacy Monuments.

I asked about doing the calligraphy, mentioning it would be the same style as the last Ellerslie Jesus Elevator verse. The man recalled the old landmark and said he had also been privileged to make Hartley Somerville's gravestone.

It was certainly not the biggest calligraphy project I have done, but it was the hardest. I wrote on it a reference to Psalm chapter

121, and focused my thoughts on the message in those verses. Many tears were shed while I worked on it, and after finalizing the template, I was exhausted—yet refreshed.

I have cried a lot since losing Mary Anne. While no one looks for reasons to cry, I cannot deny that something supernatural takes place when we release our pain, our suffering, and our tears. God surely helps those who seek him.

Mary Anne's gravestone is about thirty feet east of her parent's gravestone—my in-laws, Jan and Johanna Smits. Like all human beings, they were not perfect people, nevertheless, I consider it an honour and a privilege for Mary Anne's burial plot to be adjacent to theirs. Like my father, Jan and Johanna were also active in the Dutch resistance: risking their lives during World War II to help others. In a hiding place consisting of a false attic wall in a small townhouse, they hid friends and strangers fleeing Nazi imprisonment. It may not have been to the same scale as Corrie ten Boom's, but it was equally dangerous.

This is a photo of the bottom corner of Hartley Somerville's gravestone.

Mary Anne Vanderpyl gravestone

I Will lift up my eyes to the hills —
From whence comes my help?

My help comes from

the LORD,

Who made heaven and earth.

—Psalm 121:1,2 (NKJV)

Let the lowly brother glory in his exaltation, but the rich in his humiliation, because as a flower of the field he will pass away. For no sooner has the sun risen with a burning heat than it withers the grass; its flower falls, and its beautiful appearance perishes. So the rich man also will fade away in his pursuits. — James 1: 9-11 (NKJV)

Conduct Creates Legacy

Shortly after Mary Anne and I were married, a local church was facilitating a marriage seminar.

"Seminar," I thought, "Isn't that just a nicer way of saying counseling?" I was living a Christian life, and I had a good marriage. "Why would I need to take part in a marriage seminar?"

Some friends of ours were, however, having marital problems. "They're the ones who should be going," I figured. But I also knew that the only way he would go was if I went too. So that couple, Mary Anne, and I went to the seminar, and (surprisingly) I think I got more out of it than my friend did. The couple teaching were great actors, and their staged arguments were all-too realistic.

At one point, the man playing the role of the husband shared a scenario he refused to act out (and for obvious reasons): "If I were to ask the Pastor to stand in front of me and then went and spit on him, hitting him square in the eye, how might he react? He could make some smart remark about my aim… He could go away and pout… Or he could do what a lot of us would do, and hit me, and/or say something very nasty—But one fact remains—I did not make him mad—I only made him wet."

I had always believed the phrase: *You make me mad.*

Back then, if someone spit in my face, they would not only have made me mad, they might have made my fist sore from punching them in the nose. The idea that reactions were not determined by corresponding circumstances was foreign to me. But I could not deny the simple truth. Whether I was spit on, laughed at, annoyed, shoved or verbally abused, I was, nevertheless, the one who decided how Henry Vanderpyl (that's me) would react.

After the seminar, I stopped saying, "You make me mad," and I started taking responsibility for my reactions. Mary Anne was *very good* about reminding me if I forgot, and before long, my quick temper was left in the dust.

Remember my *little* incident at the print shop, when I was picking up the Psalm 91 scroll? God—knowing my temper was about to detonate—kindly intervened.

Though it isn't always easy to control the way we act, our conduct forms a large part of our legacy. This is why I ask myself: *Am I treating others the way I wish to be treated? Am I responding in a loving and respectful way?* And the big one: *Do I forgive those who trespass against me?*

> *The discretion of a man makes him slow to anger, and his glory is to overlook a transgression.* —Proverbs 19:11

A Treasure Waiting to be Unearthed

While writing this book, I began to think—and admittedly, for the first time—about the well-being of Mark's killer.

On the cross, Jesus died for you and me, enduring unimaginable torture and loss so we can be saved through his atoning blood. I believe this with all my heart; yet, part of me, I regret to say, has also believed that some sins—like the one committed by Mark's killer—might fall outside God's circle of grace.

"Henry," I said to myself, putting my face in my palm, "You have unforgiveness in your heart…" I took it as a personal attack that someone would have the impudence (contemptuous lack of regard for others) to blame a scripture verse for his evil actions.

I don't always reprimand myself in third person, but in this moment, I was undergoing what I call *Open-Spirit Surgery, or 'O.S.S.'* for short.

O.S.S., for most Christians, happens sometime after their S.O.S. call has been answered. It's not so much an "out-of-body experience" as it is an inner-spirit penitence. And for me, it was a stark reminder that God not only wants *my life* saved through his one and only son, Jesus—he wants *all lives* saved—including that of Mark's killer.

"Oh Lord," I prayed. "You are showing me an opportunity to show your love—your grace. I know you use all things to your good and that Your timing is perfect—mysterious—but perfect. I am Your servant, ready to do Your will."

It seems to me, whenever I am ready to do God's will, I always seem to know exactly what He wants me to do.

> *This is love, that we walk according to His command-ments. This is the commandment, that as you have heard from the beginning, you should walk in it. —2 John 6*

Right then and there, in the west Edmonton hotel room where I sat, editing this very manuscript, I grabbed a pen and began writing the letter below. And yes, I modeled it—almost word for word—on the one Corrie ten Boom wrote to the man responsible for her father and sister's capture, and subsequently, their murders. (I also included my own insights of King David—written prior to my O.S.S. procedure):

Dear Sir:

I have been writing my story about how I came to be one of the people who painted the scripture message on the Ellerslie Grain Elevator in 1979. At that time, we changed the sign from "Jesus said: There is joy in heaven over one sinner that repenteth—Luke 15" to "Jesus said: What shall it profit a man if he gain the whole world, and lose his own soul? —Mark 8."

I understand from the old news articles, that you are the one who killed a boy named Mark. I have prayed for you, that the Lord may accept you if you will repent. Think that the Lord Jesus on the Cross also took your sins upon Himself. If you accept this and want to be His child, you are saved for Eternity.

I have forgiven you in my heart, and God will also forgive you, if you ask Him. He loves you and He Himself sent His Son to earth to reconcile your sins, which meant that Jesus suffered the punishment for you and for me. You, on your part, have to give an answer to this. If He says: "Come unto Me, give Me your heart," then your answer must be: "Yes, Lord, I come, make me Your child."

If it is difficult for you to pray, then ask if God will give you His Spirit, who works the faith in your heart.

In the Bible, it tells us how King David committed adultery with Bathsheba, then arranged to have Bathsheba's husband killed to cover up his adultery. David was an adulterer and a killer.

King David's heart was broken when he came face to face with his sin, and he expressed that brokenness in Psalm 51, where he cries out to the Lord for a new nature. David genuinely wanted to be different. In verse 10, he pleads "Create in me a clean heart, O God, and renew a steadfast spirit within me. Do not cast me away from Your presence, and do not take Your Holy Spirit from me." God said that David was a man after His own heart.

King David understood the deepest human need— to have a transformed heart. It is not enough for us to simply be a better person. We need to be renewed. The Holy Spirit is able and willing to do that. If you need a life transformation, repent of your sins and pray the prayer that King David did in Psalm 51.

Never doubt the Lord Jesus' love. He is standing with His arms spread out to receive you. I hope that the path which you will now take may work for your eternal salvation.

Regards,
Henry Vanderpyl

Corrie's letter had expressed what I wanted to say to the man, who is now in his sixties, and who had hurt so many through his senseless crime.

It was important to me that God knew I was taking His task seriously, so much so, the day after writing the letter, I drove to the residence where I believed he lived: a building located a few blocks from where my wife lived when she was three or four years old.

"How great it would be if he has already repented," I thought en route to deliver the letter.

Years ago, I wrote 1 Corinthians 13—the love chapter—on a scroll. Though it isn't always easy, it is my desire, my prayer, that Jesus will help me to love other sinners—sinners whose sins are different than mine; and, when judgement starts to creep in, may I be reminded that these people need a Saviour, just as I need a Saviour.

Thankfully, *loving thy neighbour as thyself* doesn't mean we need to be neighbours to show love. Prayer—along with curious thinking—helps me pass time on the road. Would I live next door to a man like this? I wouldn't go out of my way to make it happen, I thought, but if it was God's will, I would (potentially after another round of O.S.S.) eventually align my attitude with His.

It is hard to process forgiveness. You can forgive, but you cannot forget. You shouldn't forget. If he has not been born-again, then I would be vigilant, but I would not be a vigilante. And whether or not he has been born-again, who am I to judge? *He that is without sin among you, let him first cast a stone...*

Without sin... that certainly wasn't me.

I didn't know exactly what I was going to say if he answered the door. I trusted God was going to help me with that part. If he accepted my forgiveness, and wanted to know more about salvation through Jesus, I figured I would invite him to study the Bible with me. After all, when we become born-again, we are justified from our sins. Justified means to be declared free from blame (see Romans 3:23,24). That is the power of the blood of Jesus.

Together, the man and I would move on from the past (*history*), talk about the present (*faith*, after all, is *present tense*), and about the future (*hope*) we have because Jesus has already paid the penalty for our sins.

> *He hath not dealt with us according to our sins, nor punished us according to our iniquities. For as the heavens are high above the earth, so great is His mercy toward those who fear Him; as far as the east is from the west, so far has He removed our transgressions from us. —Psalm 103: 10-12*

As it turned out, I wasn't able to gain access to the building, let alone knock on his door.

On my drive back to Coaldale, I was a little discouraged, but I also wasn't about to abandon the mission because of a logistical roadblock. I was used to this at work: sewers not being calculated at the correct depth; drainage sites not accounting for a persnickety point in a parking lot... The walls of Jericho didn't fall in a day, after all. And I suppose, a thirty-six year, *past-due* forgiveness letter could also take a bit of time to deliver.

The following Monday, I called the rental office that managed the building and was informed that the man I was trying to reach no longer lived there. Fortunately, "when God closes a door, he opens a window," and in this day and age, it's often an Internet browsing window. I was able to find out that he had moved to another city, so I obtained his correct email address and delivered the letter via email.

As told in Philippians 4:13, *I can do all things through Christ who strengthens me.* Though I made my best effort to deliver the letter by hand, part of me was relieved that the man was not around to answer the door. We don't, however, live our lives on feelings—instead, we do what we know is right to do. This was right to do. Though I haven't always complied, I want to be a man who lives to fulfill the Will of God—a man who isn't afraid to knock, and one who also isn't afraid to open up when *God* is The One knocking at the door.

At the time of publishing this book, *the man—the treasure yet to be unearthed*—has yet to respond. He might never reply. Still, I will continue praying for him whenever I think about him or whenever God puts him on my heart.

CHAPTER 7

LIVING IN THE LIGHT OF GOD'S WORD

This chapter explains some of the important things that I have learned from the Bible. It gives some background as to why I consistently have gravitated towards primarily writing scripture using my calligraphy talents.

I have taught several calligraphy classes over the years. When our oldest son, Tim, was in elementary school, I taught my calligraphy font to his grade 5/6 class. The teacher was happy to have a break and left me alone with the class during the first lesson. Writing on the blackboard with my back to the class, I turned around to see Adam Potter, my son's friend, doing somersaults.

"Get back to your seat, Adam," I said. "How's anyone going to learn with you rolling up and down the aisles?"

After three classes, to my delight, every student had a foundation to the art of calligraphy—even Adam. It did help, mind you, that I refused to turn my back to the class after the somersault incident.

Many years later, I was in contact with Adam through social media. He was living in the United States, working as a graphic artist. His interest in the field, he told me, started with that calligraphy class. I was surprised that he had retained such an interest; I would have guessed he had gone on to be a gymnast.

More than half a century after my centennial project, it has become my desire to inform people on the benefits of reading the Bible. I don't want to lecture, but instead, inspire you to seek *The Word*, so you are better prepared to withstand *The World*—and I don't intend on doing it with my back turned.

I heard some years ago: it is better to read the Bible in the morning. Why? Well, because it is better to live on it than to sleep on it. This opinion seemed to fit my experience at the time, but now I find that it is worthwhile to read the Bible anytime—anywhere.

After I accepted Jesus into my life, I appreciated the Bible so much more than in the seven prior years reading it. The Bible is God's living Word, and when utilized, provides life in return:

> *My son, give attention to my words; Incline your ear to my sayings. Do not let them depart from your eyes; Keep them in the midst of your heart; For they are life to those who find them, And health to all their flesh.*
> —*Proverbs 4:20-22*

All scripture is given by inspiration of God, and is profitable for doctrine, for reproof, for correction, for instruction in righteousness,
that the man of God may be complete, thoroughly equipped for every good work.

— 2 Tim. 3:16-17

For the word of God is living and powerful, and sharper than any two-edged sword, piercing even to the division of soul and spirit, and of joints and marrow, and is a discerner of the thoughts and intents of the heart.

— Heb. 4:12

We are overloaded with information every day. How we process it and the effect it has on us is a complicated discussion. But, one fact should not be forgotten:

> So shall My word be that goes forth from My mouth;
> It shall not return to Me void, but it shall accomplish
> what I please, and it shall prosper in the thing for which
> I sent it. —Isaiah 55:11

At the grocery store, we sometimes refer to milk, bread, eggs, and butter as the essentials, yet, they all have expiry dates. The Word of God has no expiry date. It is eternal and will not return void, which means: empty without fruit; and God's fruit never turns sour.

One Sunday in August of 2013, I visited the King of Kings Fellowship Church in the city of Lethbridge. Pastor Patty Butler's message was "The Sword of the Spirit," a term given to the Bible, based on Ephesians 6:10-20 (especially verse 17).

In the sermon, Pastor Patty made it clear that the Sword is not only our best offence, but our best defense. When we put it on the shelf and let it collect dust, it doesn't help much; but if we keep the Word of God in our minds—at all times—we are ready for everything: the good, the bad, and the ugliest of uglies.

So how can we keep the Word on our minds at all times? The easiest and hardest answer: *memorization.*

Yes, this is easier for some than for others.

One way to help memorize is to write verses on stickers and place them around the house, car, workplace... even the trees you pass while walking your dog (check your local bylaws). Some people will be able to memorize them after a few readings, and for others, it might take dozens of times. The important thing is to not get discouraged. Pray for help. God created you in His image, and that includes the magnificent design of your brain.[16]

---

16 For more on how memorization helps in life, read Psalm 119:9-11

Study, meditate on Psalm 119,
it will give you a hunger for the word of God.

The word of God:

... **helps us to change,** 119:9
How can a young man cleanse his way?
By taking heed according to <u>Your word.</u>

... **is our standard to live by,** 119:11
<u>Your word</u> I have hidden in my heart, That
I might not sin against You.

... **is our guide,** 119:30
I have chosen the way of truth.

... **has given us life,** 119:50b
For <u>Your word</u> has given me life.

... **deals well with us,** 119:65
You have dealt well with Your servant,
O LORD, according to <u>Your word.</u>

... **gives us understanding,** 119: 99, 104, 130
I have more understanding than all my
teachers, For <u>Your testimonies</u> are my
meditation. (v.99)   Through <u>Your precepts</u>
I get understanding; (v.104)   The entrance
of <u>Your words</u> gives light; it gives understanding to the simple. (v.130)

... **gives us direction and guidance,** 119:105
<u>Your word</u> is a lamp to my feet And a light
to my path.

The entirety of <u>Your word</u>
is truth, (v. 160a)

We need to live according to the Word, keeping the Will of God at the forefront of our minds. In the hour of battle, when temptation is at the door, we have to live in the Word; and if the Sword does not have mastery over us, the world will.[17]

Sporadic note scribbling while listening to a sermon doesn't necessarily capture the entire message, but if I could emphasize just one Pastor-Patty-Bible-reading-tip, it would be this: *memorize scripture.* Satan does not wait until we are ready to attack; for this reason, we all would benefit in having key Bible verses readily available in our hearts and minds so we can *reply* and *resist* by the power of the Sword.

Remember the scene in Star Wars where Luke Skywalker is beginning to feel and use the Force? Here he is, onboard the Millenium Falcon, wearing a goofy, sci-fi version of a blindfold, doing his best to avoid being shot by a laser-zapping robot. "Remember, a Jedi can feel the Force flowing through him," Obi-Wan tells him as he gets shot in the leg.

In a (more practical) way, the Bible, when read regularly, is a force that flows through us. A force we can feel and use—and as much as we want. With it, we can defend ourselves from temptation; we can cut through lies, and we can also spread light. (It's no wonder they named them lightsabers...)

> *Your word is a lamp to my feet and a light to my path.*
> *–Psalm 119:105*

When you go into a dark room and turn on the lights, what happens? Darkness flees at the speed of light. In the same way, the Spirit of God enters a room whenever a Bible is opened. Another fun tidbit... the Bible is the only book you can read with the Author present every time you open it.

---

17   For more on winning the battle of temptation, read Matthew 4:1-25.

When someone is born again, God breathes into them a new life. Did you know—our born-again spirit is actually meant to be our boss. Still, something inside our (sinful) genetic makeup will try (and try and try and try) to take back control in a never-ending effort to steal our God-given freedom.

Reading the Bible on a daily basis is not legalism. Nor is it a routine safety drill, like the ones you might have to do at work or school. It is, however, self-discipline.

> *If you abide in My word, you are My disciples indeed.*
> *And you shall know the truth, and the truth shall make*
> *you free. —John 8:31b-32*

For this reason, we cannot simply agree that God's Word reigns supreme over our lives, we must take every possible measure to consume and retain it. We have to take responsibility for our actions—for our thoughts. Thankfully, the Bible not only tells us how we should live, but how we should think.

> *Finally, brethren, whatever things are true, whatever*
> *things are noble, whatever things are just, whatever*
> *things are pure, whatever things are lovely, whatever*
> *things are of good report, if there is any virtue and if*
> *there is anything praiseworthy—meditate on these*
> *things. —Philippians 4:8*

The Trending De-Emphasis of God's Word

While sorting through various calligraphy files, plaques and projects—which would require a library coding system to keep track of—I realized that the walls of my home did not have near as much scripture as they once had, say thirty to thirty-five years ago.

I pondered this while touring my home and discovered an interesting reality. I have a stick-on decal on my front door that reads:

> Welcome To Our Home,
> As for me and my house, we will serve the Lord. –
> Joshua 24:15b

That sentence is actually the end of verse 15; earlier in the verse it says, "Choose for yourselves this day whom you will serve," then continues, "but as for me and my house, we will serve the Lord." When interviewing Alice Somerville, she told me how Hartley's version of writing God's Word on the doorframe of his house was to go one step bigger and put it on a grain elevator.

Entering my home, you are immediately greeted (after me) by the Psalm 91 scroll I have on display. Aside from this, there are (admittedly) not near as many verses on my walls and fridge as there once were, and for someone who's gift and hobby is scripture-calligraphy, I have no excuse.

Most of my friends once displayed similar decals, scrolls, and plaques, but today, I can count them on one hand. Similarly, whether or not a Christian decorated with scripture, most Christ-centred homes had a Bible in plain sight, or at least they knew where to find it, when asked. My Bible also used to be in plain view, but in recent years—and not necessarily because I'm afraid someone may steal it—I have kept it tucked away, out of sight. And, we all know how the old saying goes: "Out of sight—out of mind."

As much as the Bible or a verse may simply be a display (and for some, a way to suck up to Grandma), they are, more importantly, frequent visual reminders to read God's Word. If they are not in our sight, they are not in our hands, and when they are not *in* our hands—they are not *on* our hearts.[18]

For many, shelves and interior walls are a place to display photos of family, friends, and pets; backdrops for art and/or nostalgic souvenirs; storyboards of the characters and settings we hold most dear—unless that thing is money—nobody should cover their walls with that. Yes, whatever we choose to display in our homes, one thing is for sure: our walls, shelves, coffee tables, and fridges, and more so, the things we put on them—are a wonder to ourselves. (Holes, fingerprints, food and dust not included.)

So, what do you hang upon your walls? What do you affix to your fridge, or rest upon your coffee and bedside tables? Do you have a Bible on display? Or like mine did, has it found a hiding place?

These days, our phones are so smart, there are few questions we can't instantly find answers to. This includes several great Bible apps, which not only include God's Word, but daily reading plans, devotionals, and countless study aids. This is great. Truly. Still, when I open my preferred Bible app in church, it is all too easy to get distracted. The same device offering digitized insights from God also hosts a Pandora-sized screen of other *useful* apps, designed to lure our minds and souls into an endless game of red-notification whack-a-mole. I call it *DDD* (Digital Device Dependent); and expect these distractions to continue as long as I use my smartphone as a Bible.

---

18   See Deuteronomy 6:6-9.

What if?

... Our Bible was just as important as our cell phone?

What if?...

... we treated it like we couldn't live without it?

.. when we forgot it, we went back to get it?

... we always had it close by in case of an emergency?

...we made sure our battery never ran low?

...we checked it throughout the day for new messages?

Jesus said: "...If you abide in My word, you are My disciples indeed. And you shall know the truth, and the truth shall make you free." —John 8:31b-32 (NKJV)

Effect of Displaying God's Word

A family friend told me her daughter, after becoming a teenager, was asked to write her testimony. The teen told her mom she would often read the scripture plaque in her room and one day, after praying the sinner's prayer, asked Jesus to forgive her sins, and that is how she became born-again.

> But what does it say? "The word is near you, in your mouth and in your heart" (that is, the word of faith which we preach): that if you confess with your mouth the Lord Jesus and believe in your heart that God has raised Him from the dead, you will be saved. For with the heart one believes unto righteousness, and with the mouth confession is made unto salvation. — Romans 10:8-10

And every time you hear and obey the Word of God, it is accompanied by faith:

> *So then faith comes by hearing, and hearing by the word of God. —Romans 10:17*

Why display scripture? Because what you focus on—is what you give power to. Listen to God's Word so that you won't be trapped, misled, or deceived by the other voices. The more pressure you have coming at you from the outside, the more you need support from the Holy Spirit inside you.

In one of the engineering offices I worked in, the secretary was going through challenges in her marriage. Then her husband passed away, and she became the single parent to their daughter. She was a Christian and went to church regularly, but she was often overwhelmed by single-parenthood. On several occasions, seeing that she was visibly distressed, I took a sticky note and wrote a Bible verse on it.[19] I then stuck the note to her desk or computer monitor. Years later, she let me know how much they ministered to her in her time of need. She was even thinking of laminating them—something I thought was reserved for school teachers and recipe collectors. God's Word is powerful and worth sharing.

I learned something from this, when I give someone a card (for sympathy or celebration), I try to include a Bible verse. Not always, but at least when I feel God whispering into my ear—and out my pen.

---

19   Such as Proverbs 3:5,6; Philippians 4:13; II Timothy 1:7; Matthew 6:33,34

Mind on Task

Currently, I am self-employed, working as an engineer/technologist designing and inspecting the construction of sewer collection systems, water distribution systems, drainage, and roadways for new or revitalized subdivision developments.

Sharing with a colleague how I was working on safety protocols for myself, he told me that one of the major oil sands developments he was working on in northern Alberta has various cultural backgrounds represented among the workers. For this reason, a lot of effort goes into making their safety protocols usable and understood. "Still," he continued, "it all boils down to three words to describe the safety emphasis in its lowest common denominator. Whether you work in an office or on a major construction site, you must focus your thinking, close out distractions, and keep your *mind on task*.

From time to time, when I lose focus, I feel myself floating through life, one errand to the next—which is no way to live. Whether I am at home, work, church, the grocery store or the movies, I owe it to myself, my family, my colleagues, my fellow believers, and the strangers I pass in the aisle and on the road—to be present, to be purposeful, and to be prepared for the unexpected plans and promptings of the Holy Spirit. Distracted driving is not only a danger behind the wheel, it's a dangerously-sure way to miss destiny's next turn.

Since becoming a Christian, asking for directions has never been easier. No matter how many turns I miss, I know I can always come back to God, and—through prayer and reading the Bible—refocus my *mind on task*.

installation of garbage bins downtown. Great idea, except she had not consulted with the one person she needed to before approving the cost: me. Historically, there had already been a lot of friction between the recreation and public works departments, and knowing I have a much higher well-received-reaction ratio *after* collecting my thoughts, I decided I would wait things out. A couple of weeks went by before Madame Récreation, as I'll call her, stopped by my office to ask if I had noticed the garbage containers her staff had installed along the town's main street.

"I noticed." I said.

To which, she (abruptly) replied, "It will only take your crew five minutes a day to check and empty them."

"And where, do you suppose, I will get the extra $1,000 for my budget?" I said. "I don't need a calculator to figure it out. Five minutes per day times twenty working days per month is twelve hundred minutes per year, or twenty hours production time. My hard costs for just the operators' wages and fuel to run the truck are about $50/hour—multiply that by twenty, and I'm accounting for an extra $1,000."

After an awkward, yet satisfying silence, I told her my crew would do the pick-ups, but to ask me first—should our calculators and spreadsheets cross paths again.

God created people, math—and people to do math—and saw that it was good. This event parallels our personal lives, doesn't it? How seemingly small things, like watching TV and excessively checking our phones, have their costs. Sometimes we should add things to our schedule and budget. My children took piano lessons when they were young, which cost money, time, and a piano to practice on. But these lessons helped my children to develop routine discipline, a love of music, and an ability to worship God through melodious finger strokes. Time and money well spent.

On other occasions, there are things in our lives that do not warrant our time and money, and which should be immediately decreased, if not entirely removed. Most people (myself included) spend a lot more than five minutes a day checking (and rechecking) their electronic devices. But, as garbage collection proves, even small numbers add up. If I spend just five minutes a day reading the Bible, I will gain thirty hours of *God* in a year.

The problem with good, simple principles, however, is that by simply replacing a few variables, we can turn them into a labyrinth of bad. For example, if I also spend an hour watching or listening to less-than-holy media every day, the same principle tells me I will gain three hundred and sixty-five hours of *The World*, and arguably—wrong instruction. Whether it is viewing a few of the billion YouTube videos uploaded every day, having read the Jesus Elevator verses on your morning and evening commutes throughout 1965 to 1989, or repeatedly declaring upon your return home: "As for me and my house, we shall serve the Lord"—they have a cumulative effect on us.

Seeing the world shifting from God's Word is what motivated me to write this book. I don't read the Bible because it is the bestselling book in the world. Nor do I read it because it is easy. In fact, it is very hard to do—consistently—and I expect I may struggle with it until the day I die.

Nevertheless, I return to the Bible, time and time again, because it is my only earthly possession that can bring me closer to my one, true God. As the first verse in the book of John states: "In the beginning was the Word, and the Word was with God, and the Word was God." *The Word was God*... does that mean that spending time in the Word is the same as spending time with God?

It certainly does.

And when you spend time with God, you not only go places, you go places where He wants to take you. The Bible, after all, is life's one true compass; it always points north, and it never fails to give direction. Moreover, reciting and singing its verses is like connecting a straw to heaven (a biodegradable one, I'm sure...)

And, who in their right mind, you might ask, would have a straw to Heaven and only drink from it once? I hope I speak for most people when I say, "nobody." For this reason, we ought to drink His Word daily—or better yet—as much and as often as we can.

And these words which I command you today shall be in your heart. You shall teach them diligently to your children, and shall talk of them when you sit in your house, when you walk by the way, when you lie down, and when you rise up. You shall bind them as a sign on your hand, and they shall be as frontlets between your eyes. You shall write them on the doorposts of your house and on your gates. —Deuteronomy 6:6-9

CHAPTER 8

LIFE'S JOURNEY HOLDING A CALLIGRAPHY PEN

We Live by Faith

Considering both the Old and New Testament, the Jesus Elevator ministered only two of the Bible's 31,102 verses. There is limitless depth to the Bible, including our Saviour's origins; our present living compared to the days before and shortly after Christ; and God's plan (dates unknown) for our future—and more so, from an eternal perspective.

We serve an infinite God who has dominion over everything, yet He is willing to help us through our day-to-day—without diminishing His ability to help those with more pressing needs.

Writing this book has coincided with my grief-riddled road to accepting Mary Anne's death. The journey has been anything but easy, but the power of prayer and the wisdom of God's word has made the process possible, and I am happy to share what I have learned and what I still hope to learn.

> *But we all, with unveiled face, beholding as in a mirror the glory of the Lord, are being transformed into the same image from glory to glory, just as by the Spirit of the Lord.* —2 Corinthians 3:18

The Word of God is key for spiritual nourishment; each verse a kernel of grain making up the bread of life. Obviously, we need much more than one kernel to make a loaf of bread. Trust me—I grew up in a bakery...

Like my own journey to healing, there is a process for seeds to grow and for grain to produce, and for us, part of that process is prayer. Throughout most of my life, I have used *arrow-prayers* for myself, my family and others. My Dutch surname, van der Pijl, means *from the Arrow*, but you don't need the namesake to shoot an arrow prayer. When you have a genuine relationship with the Lord, you are consumed by His love.

I shoot arrow thoughts—not just thoughts, but short prayers shot to heaven—in everyday situations: big and small. Before his wife went shopping, Hartley Somerville would ask her if she remembered to pray about where she was going to park. He prayed about everything. I think about everything, and I am trying to send more arrows. Come to think of it, these are probably the types of prayers Pastor Hertzsprung *shot* for me and my siblings.

> *Most assuredly, I say to you, unless a grain of wheat falls into the ground and dies, it remains alone; but if it dies, it produces much grain.* —John 12:24

The Power of Prayer

I have learned to not underestimate the power of prayer.

In 2016, returning home on Christmas Eve after a wonderful Christmas celebration with all our children and grandchildren, coming over a small hill, Mary Anne and I encountered a major highway accident. We could tell right away that it was serious. First on the scene, we observed (in horror): seven people trapped in crumpled metal, two dead, and another who would succumb to her injuries by the next day. I assisted where I could, and other people soon (it felt like forever) stopped to help until the ambulances and fire trucks arrived. That vehicle accident closed Highway 3, a major highway, for over five hours while the emergency responders completed the extrications and clean-up.

For the next few weeks, I did not sleep well. Night after night, I woke up thinking of the two girls in the backseat who had lost their parents and sister in the accident. After catching my breath, I would pray for them. They were about the same age as my daughters, and my heart was broken for them. I still use arrow prayers when I think of them and the emergency responders.

Three weeks after that accident, Mary Anne passed away. It was not just a difficult time—it was *the most* difficult time, and I thank God for my children, friends and extended family whose prayers, biblical wisdom, and above all—love—that carried me through.

Mary Anne had a gift for remembering people, their names and how they were connected to one another. Essentially, she was Facebook before Facebook was invented. Her funeral was attended by more than five hundred people, which did not surprise me. I wanted to give a eulogy to honour her, and, approaching the platform, I thought, "How could I not do this? I have so many people praying for me." There is power in prayer, and my six children and I (miraculously) held ourselves together. That includes my special needs son.

We are not promised to have everything easy in life, but Jesus is our ever-present promise in times of trouble.[23]

In life, the world around us, and the individuals in our lives will move us to prayer. Hartley Somerville, I was told, often mentioned his brother Walter when he prayed, and also asked others to pray for Walter. Hartley thought of others first, and knowing where he was going, was particularly concerned for his brother's spiritual well-being. Right up until he passed away, Hartley continued praying for Walter; and true to Luke 15, he got to celebrate his brother's repentance shortly after leaving this world—and in Heaven no less.

Our God is big enough to minister to individuals—an entire world of individuals—so we ought to maintain a giving spirit when it comes to praying for others. When God gives you a burden to pray for somebody, He is also making a promise that, in his timing, your prayer will be answered—and not necessarily in the way you expect. Our God is not only big, He's mysterious too, and so are his ways.

Part of living in the present tense is to be in season and out of season with our prayer life. Living in the present includes an attitude of not giving up.

> *Preach the word! Be ready in season and out of season, Convince, rebuke, exhort, with all longsuffering and teaching. —2 Timothy 4:2*

---

23   See Psalm 46:1

Rejoice always, pray without ceasing, in everything give thanks; for this is the will of God in Christ Jesus for you.

— 1 Thessalonians 5:16-18

The above verses in I Thessalonians support a prayer and praise-filled lifestyle. Just as breakfast and exercise are parts of a healthy way of life, prayer and gratitude are essential to a healthy, spiritual relationship with God. God loves when we communicate with Him—when we trust Him, and thank Him, and when we unselfishly pray for others.

Before I was saved, Mr. Hertzsprung prayed for me. Hartley, likewise, prayed regularly, not just for his siblings, but for those reading and thinking about the verses on his elevator—for the unsaved.

When you eat, you are responding to the cries of your stomach. When you pray and give thanks, you are obeying the Will of God. Don't underestimate the power of prayer—instead, feed your soul daily—because, how can you help feed others if you yourself are starving?

Writing Names in Bibles is a Ministry?

When it occurred to me that I could start ministering by writing people's names in their Bibles, a ministry of small beginnings was born. Soon, I was asked to write—and sometimes, in expensive Bibles—a person's favourite verse. Then came a sizeable scroll for displaying a whole chapter of God's Word. And later, large (gigantic) posters and banners for various Christian events, other unique calligraphy projects, and then, my pièce de résistance: the second Jesus Elevator verse.

Recently, two young-adult siblings were getting married in the summer (yes, to different people) and their request to their parents was that they each wanted a nice, large Bible for their respective homes. As I wrote their names in the Bibles, I knew God was already relevant to their relationships. I also knew that— while the pots, pans, toaster oven and cutlery on their registries would help them feed themselves—only the Bible could help them feed their souls.

God's Word is as relevant today as it was when Moses and the Israelites crossed the Red Sea; when David triumphed over Goliath before becoming King; when Hartley bought, moved and repurposed an elevator; when I, Henry Vanderpyl, decided to write a book, and in the process, faced (once more) my biggest fears, hurts, and feelings of unforgiveness—my weaknesses and hypocrisy in daily pursuing and reflecting the love of Christ. God's Word was relevant, is relevant, and will always be relevant. Put it up next to any book—it remains the most relevant message for all history, for all time, and for all eternity.

Throughout my life, I have struggled to comprehend God's infinite size, existence, knowledge and power. Then again, it is hard for the finite to understand the Infinite. At least it can be, up until the Infinite reveals Himself. This is what the Bible does—it reveals the love and character of our Creator.[24]

A recent survey revealed a high percentage of Christians don't feel responsible for sharing the gospel.[25] This is contrary to scripture. The great commission was not just assigned to the church, it was assigned to each and every one of us who believes.

From Basement Suite Wall-Covering to Around-the-World Distribution

The Psalm 91 scroll made for Penny's basement suite was reproduced for distribution using sepia paper or blueprinting, which were both susceptible to moisture damage, and tore easily. Years later, I decided to silk-screen it onto cloth so it would be more durable. But at the silk screen shop, I was told it couldn't be done: "It can't be done," they said. "Nobody silk-screens anything *that* big."

They weren't wrong. Fifteen by forty-one inches (the size of the scroll) would have been the equivalent size of a dreadfully long T-shirt—so I wasn't totally surprised by their response. Nevertheless, I still believed the scroll could *and should* be silk-screened, so I kept searching, I kept asking… Eventually, I was directed to Mr. Sim Woods, a retired man with silk-screening experience. He fabricated larger-than-normal screens, assembled six spotlights into a frame and—in an improvised dark room in his garage—exposed the film onto his creation. The result: silk-screened scrolls on cloth—more durable and easier to ship—and, as far as I'm concerned, the *finest* invention of 1982 (the year the

---

24   This is not just a hard concept for children, it's hard for people of all ages. Read the book of Job to better understand who God is and what He is capable of.

25   Research conducted by the Barna Group: https://www.barna.com/research/sharing-faith-increasingly-optional-christians/

first CD player was sold, and the same year Times Magazine gave its "Man of the Year" award to a computer).

Sim and I shared a desire for getting scripture into peoples' homes—and at a reasonable cost. I also made scrolls (all in King James, which complimented my Olde English style) for First Corinthians 13 (the "love chapter"), Psalm 23 (The Lord is my Shepherd), as well as a Dutch version of the Psalm 91 scroll—which I would still love to letter onto a pair of wooden shoes... *Big* shoes.

The scrolls, which involved silk screening, sewing the borders, assembling dowels and scroll knobs, attaching the string, (neatly) packing them up and (cost-effectively) shipping them out—required a fair bit of labour and repetitive discipline. Over the years, I sold or gave away more than nine-hundred scrolls in various formats—*literally* distributing the Word of God around the world (some as far as Thailand for missionary gifts).

Unfortunately, a few years into the venture, Sim passed away, the scroll knob supplier went out of business, and my silk-screen scroll-assembly shop slipped into a deep sleep. Although I never made a significant profit selling (and giving away) scrolls (the business was, admittedly, a labour of love), I would have kept the business running as long as God told me to. It did help, mind you, that I knew it wasn't so much a *business* as it was a ministry—my obedience to the Great Commission—extending God's Word into the lives of those who faithfully displayed, read and memorized it.[26]

And, though I know that even cloth will one day fade away, my faith rests in the everlasting message that will last for eternity.

---

26 A few years after Sim Woods passed away, I taught a calligraphy class at the Crowsnest Lake Bible Camp. As I set up the teaching area with various samples that included the scrolls, I looked out the window and noticed a dormitory cabin named "The Woods"—named after Sim. Part of a legacy recognition, but I think more importantly, a tribute to someone who helped get God's Word onto the walls of homes around the world—where scriptures can be read and re-read until memorized.

The Operator's Manual

I like the idea of our Bible being *The Operator's Manual* of operator manuals—and not just because I'm one of the few guys who actually keeps these little booklets handy. Operator manuals, I concede, have become a bit retro, with more and more people preferring concise online videos and forums. No extras, just meat-and-potato answers—made to order and served up in thirty seconds or less.

Information contained in typical operator manuals include:
- Safety instructions, including warnings against increased wear-and-tear;
- Instructions for *intended* operations;
- Programming and maintenance instructions;
- Product technical specs;
- Frequently Asked Questions;
- and the big one: *Warranty.*

When we consult our Manual in good times, we are being diligent and faithful operators. When we consult it in difficult times, we are allowing God to be God—the best, most trustworthy *Mechanic* in the universe—and, in turn, refuel our relationship with Him.

In choosing Christ, we are instantly connected to God and the promise He has made for us. As you continue to read His Word, continue to seek who you are and who you were made to be—and not just in mind and body—but in spirit.

So, what does the Bible say about me, you ask?

If you truly want to know, there are no videos or forums you can skip to. Although you can access a fully-indexed list of frequently asked questions, and with a bit of guesswork, get a general idea of how you tick—or how you can be fixed if you're feeling broken—there's no shortcut to a two-way relationship with the Creator of the Universe. Even if you have memorized every commandment and every verse, Jesus is neither impressed nor convinced by your knowledge of the Bible. In fact, the only way to convince Him that you are His and He is yours is by spending time with Him—the good, old fashioned way: no shortcuts—no quick fixes.[27]

When I meditate on the Word, I speak over myself the way I hear God speaking over me. I know when I am in tune with who I am in God—I will also be in tune with what God is *speaking* over me, and duly so—over every person I am praying for.

The Bible is big, and—when read by a human—cannot be absorbed in one reading. Even so, the most important part of anything valuable—is its warranty. Thank goodness we don't need to understand everything about God's grace to receive it. We simply need to be born again.

Jesus is not only our written guarantee, He's our living one. And, best of all, His promise never expires.

---

27 See Matthew 7:7-27

CHAPTER 9

ALONG THE ROAD TO ETERNITY

All Roads Lead to the Cross

In the mid-1980's, I lived in Lloydminster, a city straddling the border of Alberta and Saskatchewan. Working as an engineer, I looked after the survey, design, and onsite inspection of problem roadways in the Cold Lake First Nations Reserve. To get there, I often took Secondary Highway 897 for a hundred fifty kilometers (with about half that distance being on gravel roads). Dealing with the washboard effects of gravel roads was an ongoing struggle and maintenance and reconstruction was an ongoing process.

This commute meant, especially after a bit of rain, I had to drive slowly—earning myself many hours of solitary time behind the wheel. To keep me in God's Word—key to living a Christian life—I plastered my dashboard with notes, verses, and biblical truths. Mary Anne, most likely seeing the dangers of reading while driving, encouraged me to start listening to Bible CD's on my trips.

It was a great idea, and during one such trip—listening to Ephesians chapter 5, I kept rewinding and replaying verses 25 and 26. Like deer bolting out of the ditch, they were jumping out at me. Replaying them several more times, I realized they carried a relevant message for me as a husband.

> *Husbands, love your wives, just as Christ also loved the church and gave Himself for her, that He might sanctify and cleanse her with the washing of water by the word.*
> *—Ephesians 5:25-26*

In hindsight, I'm sure God was ensuring Mary Anne's CD suggestion would not only refine me as a Christian, but as a husband, too.

Prior to life in Lloydminster, I attended a Bible study where we discussed the symbolism of the Mosaic tabernacle. (The Mosaic tabernacle is described in Exodus 25:8 to 27:21). When reconstructing an aerial view of this portable tabernacle that was set up during the Biblical exodus; its furnishings (Altar, Laver, Altar of Incense, Ark of the Covenant, Candlestick, and Table of Showbread) form a distinct cross-shaped pattern. If you look at the numbers for each of the twelve tribes, you realize that the Israelites also camped in a pattern of the cross.

Studying this, I noted that the Laver, the least described furnishing (scripture simply states that it was made from the mirrors of the women—see Exodus 30:18-21), was a large basin used for ceremonial washings—a place where the priests were required to wash their hands and feet before ministering in the Holy Place (the inner court).

Equipped with this knowledge, I was able to truly hear God through Ephesians 5:26, which, for me, was speaking about leadership at home. A husband is accountable not only to God, but to his wife. He shows caution to this spiritual responsibility through the "washing of water by the word."

A husband who regularly washes in the word, I realized, also makes it easier for his wife, the mirror-made Laver, to submit to his leadership, and in turn, reflect the same spiritual cleanliness.

These verses were a breakthrough in how I listened to and interpreted the Bible. By immersing myself in the Word of God, I have been able to wash away the stains of the world before going deeper into ministry—at home, and beyond.

Working and driving on countless roadways, it has also come to my attention that at every crossroads intersection a cross is formed. There, on life's loneliest roads, Jesus is there for us: at every gravel washboard—at every pothole, swerve and surprise, and every head-on collision.

He is the way, the truth and the life. He is the surveyor, the engineer, and the reconstruction crew—and there are no roads too troublesome for our God to fix.

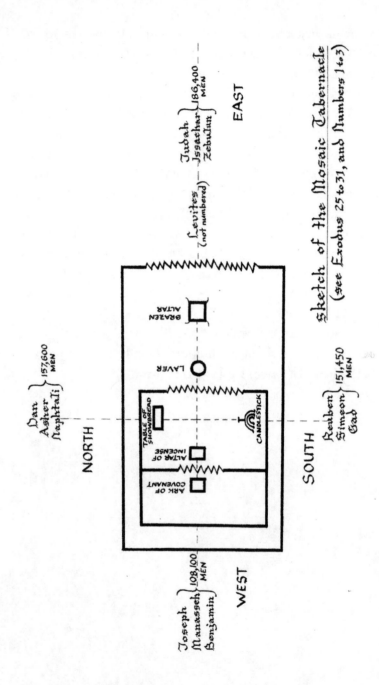

Sketch of the Mosaic Tabernacle
(see Exodus 25 to 31, and Numbers 1 to 3)

At the Foot of the Cross

Though the Tabernacle's outer court was accessible to *whosoever* entered by its gate (at the foot of the cross), only the (fully-atoned) High Priest could enter the Holy of Holies. The first furnishing on display was the Brazen Altar, reminding *whosoever* that they were not worthy to proceed any further without a proper animal sacrifice.

As an engineer, I found it fascinating that one of God's altars could be a hardwood box, overlain with brass. These materials sounded like the right components for a fire-resistant door, but an Altar? Animals were brought five at a time: four of them tied to the horns of the Altar, one at each corner, while the fifth was sacrificed.

The full Exodus detailing of the Mosaic Tabernacle is interesting (and thoroughly written), but with the New Testament, we are no longer *tied* to the Altar (except by our own will). *Whosoever will,* may come to Jesus—at the foot of the cross—and receive His free gift of salvation.

The Tabernacle and Temple represent similar blueprints that people consult. These plans, when followed correctly, guide our hands and minds, and help direct our lives. The Bible, a multi-layered blueprint that only God fully understands, was created for this same purpose. Like my prized Psalm 91 scroll, ruined in the roller, we—as operators—must keep our eyes on the prize, our minds *on task*, and the Word of God, ever present in our lives.

It is no coincidence that the Mosaic Tabernacle foretold God's plans of *The Cross*. Though an endless slaughter of lambs and sheep upon the brazen altar were required to satisfy God's Old Testament, Jesus, as the *one-and-only* sacrificial lamb, broke the gates, once and for all, wide-open to His loving Father's New, Eternal Testament. He didn't spend his time thinking about the here and now—he focused on the Will of His Father—the forever and until.

Today, we are in the New Testament (New Covenant) and whosoever seeks to enter Heaven only needs to repent and accept Jesus. First comes life, then we face eternity. Jesus died on the cross so that we can be saved. The old testament foretold that Jesus would die on a cross.

The Domino Effect of Human Dynamos

It's no coincidence the first word on the elevator is Jesus. It's no coincidence George Bradley had to stretch out from the *comfort* of the swing scaffold to hammer on the top portion of the "J". It's no coincidence Jesus is—and needs to be—always at the top— the name above all names. Though too often in my life, I have struggled to stay in His word, Jesus has been—and will always be—victorious in my life.

While writing this book, I wrote a list of items that Hartley and I had in common or in parallel. At the risk of sounding self-centered, I have decided to list them.

Consider the following (third-person) parallels:
- Hartley Somerville wanted people to realize the truth and perspective of the verse that is repeated twice in Luke 15. Henry Vanderpyl viewed the first grain elevator message on a regular basis and was reading that same scripture, which helped him put his life into perspective and answer the altar call. Although Hartley was a successful man, he kept his motivation to share the gospel freely. He knew what Mark 8:36 means; and kept his life in a Biblical perspective.

- Hartley had prior experience owning and working with grain elevators—he understood them. He also had previous heavy construction equipment experience which enabled him to "drag" the elevator building over to his farm property using his own bulldozer. Henry had prior experience working with painting tradesmen and previous experience painting very large signs and banners.

- Hartley and Henry both had relatively large families—six kids each, and you need Biblical help to father a larger family. Both prayed regularly and realized that the Word of God is important to read, study, and share to direct themselves and to stay on the right path in life.

- Hartley and Henry had parallel motivations to see the scriptures put on public display—to shine a spotlight on the gospel message for others. Why would someone want to put a Scripture verse on display? To share the Good News! Both had a reverent respect for God's Word, and both called themselves Christians, each making his decision to follow Jesus at age twenty-two and wishing they had done so earlier in life.

- Hartley did not hesitate to do things in a big way during his career. Together with his brother Walter, he became one of the Flax Kings in the farming circles, helped build part of the trans-Canada Highway, and even moved a full-sized grain elevator with his own bulldozer. Henry did not hesitate to do calligraphy in a big way over the years starting with large five-foot scrolls, fifteen by twenty-five foot posters at the U of A, the ninety-nine-foot banner for a Crusade, street banners spanning streets, and then the second Jesus Elevator verse with *small (lower case)* letters measuring 20" high. They each had their gifts, and both were not hesitant to apply them on big projects. The result was the largest scripture sign ever displayed in Canada—a

Lighthouse message on the Prairies—during the years 1965 to 1989.

- Hartley and Mary Anne's gravestones were done by the same monument company, Legacy Monuments. The locations of both graveyards and the location of the landmark Jesus Elevator are, all three, within close proximity to the east side of Highway 2.

- There are parallels in Hartley and Henry's background lives that were complementary to effectively accomplish the second Jesus Elevator verse that made a difference in many lives because it spread the message of the scriptures, encouraging people to prepare themselves for eternity.

If you ask the question, "Who was behind the Jesus Elevator," the answer is Hartley Somerville. Henry and George just did the calligraphy for the second message. A lot of people combined their efforts, work and time, including finances, to put the scriptures on display, and a calligraphy hobby became just one part of its legacy. The verses displayed were not only appropriate for the Edmonton region—the Gateway to the North—but for Christians in Canada, and to the ends of the Earth (Canada's international calling).

Whatever your gifts are, pray about how you can use them to help fulfill the Great Commission. Our talents are more meaningful when they are partnered with the Holy Spirit, sharing the same goal of shining a light upon God's glory and the pathway to spending eternity with Him.

I'm Looking at the Man in the Laver

As I reflect on my own journey, I see the various preparations, provisions, grooming, and training required to be successful, and not only at work, but in all aspects of life. Jesus told His followers:

> ... I am going there (to Heaven) to prepare a place for you. And if I go and prepare a place for you, I will come back and take you to be with me that you also may be where I am. —John 14:2,3 (NIV)

To prepare is to put oneself in readiness for a new situation or condition. You can prepare yourself for defeat or prepare yourself for victory. As I reflect on the preparation of God's Word in my life, the preparation of my calligraphy calling, including my desire to "Go Big," and the preparation and painting of the elevator, I see that God used it all to share His love.

How could the messages on the Jesus Elevator ever be overshadowed by servants of darkness? It cannot.

> For our struggle is not against flesh and blood, but against the rulers, against the authorities, against the powers of this dark world and against the spiritual forces of evil in the heavenly realms. —Ephesians 6:12 NIV

How did Corrie ten Boom go through her times of trouble? By applying God's Word, including Psalm 91—*In the shadow of El Shaddai* (God Almighty, the All-sufficient One). God gave me a word of knowledge to ease my anger when the original Psalm 91 scroll was destroyed. It was preparing my heart to get through times of trouble and disappointment.

Being born-again is a relationship, not a religious ritual.

I press toward the mark for the prize of the high calling
of God in Christ Jesus. —Philippians 3:14 (KJV).

That is my goal—my purpose—propelling me closer to Jesus.

What purpose is propelling you closer to Jesus? What is pulling
you away?

To live in the Shadow of El-Shaddai is to also live in the Light of the Lord. Like the Jesus Elevator, we too can shine a light for others, not only by displaying the Word of God, but by displaying His Spirit in the way we talk, the way we walk, and the way we pray.

You and I were not created in error. Our God does not make mistakes. Your life, your talents, your wins and your losses—reading the scriptures in this book—are all things that declare you are on the right path, that your mind is on task, and that you are aiming at the high calling of God in Christ Jesus.

Though Hartley's elevator was originally built to house grain, it was *repurposed* to house hope and shine light. This is my prayer for you—that no matter your circumstances, God will continue His work in you. Whoever you think you may be, God knows who you are meant to be, and not just for this life, but all eternity.

In the days ahead, may you stay in God's word, may it stay in your heart, on your mind, and when you feel His prompting, may you release it into the world, sharing it with whosoever will listen.

Calligraphy, as always—optional.

EPILOGUE

Though I have enjoyed reliving the resurrection of the Jesus Elevator in my life, I admit, I didn't always feel like writing. The same has been true for my walk with Christ and my meditating on His Word.

In this book, I have provided scriptural context to help frame the story inside the Jesus Elevator. I also want to share the Good News of the gospel, but I don't want the reader to feel "ambushed" by the sermon-like notes, so I have provided them in the Appendix as optional reading.

Thanks very much for reading. I hope you continue to search your Bible to get to know God.

Stay tuned for future calligraphy and stories in my next book, and on my website.

APPENDIX

DON'T WANT NO HAND-ME-DOWN RELIGION

Jesus did not like religion.

There is a big difference between wanting more *of* God over wanting more *from* God. In this life, there is nothing I need more *of* than God. There is more to Him than I know. He is infinite. For this reason, I must remain hungry. I must thirst for what matters most.

When Jesus spoke to the Pharisees, Sadducees, and Scribes, he was straightforward, humble and meek. He saw right through their religion, their hypocrisy, and their pride.

When I was in my mid-twenties, I hosted a Bible Study in my home. I was in a position of leadership and felt responsible for keeping the discussions within the context of the Bible. At one of the studies, a two-week-old, born-again Christian started the evening by saying he had a question about regularly going to church. I thought to myself, "Oh no, the discussion hasn't even begun, and it's already off track." He then went on to say how the answer was in his Bible all along:

> *So He came to Nazareth, where He had been brought up. And as His custom was, He went into the synagogue on the Sabbath day, and stood up to read. —Luke 4:16*

"If Jesus showed the example of attending the synagogue regularly, that is the example we should also follow," he concluded. I thought to myself, how can you argue against that?

George Bradley once told me, "Henry, if you find a perfect church, don't join it—you will *ruin* it," and for thirty years, I attended a church whose slogan was, "No perfect people allowed." I fit right in.

I have always identified with people who struggle to live a Christian life. For this reason, I still remember a bumper sticker that said it best: "Christians are not perfect, just forgiven." Religion does not get you into heaven—being born again does.

> *Jesus answered and said to him, "Most assuredly, I say to you, unless one is born again, he cannot see the kingdom of God." –John 3:3*

Both heaven and hell are real places. And it's my direction—not my intention—that determines which one I ultimately go to. Most people don't like thinking about hell. I don't either. But just because we rather not talk or think about it, doesn't mean it's not there, waiting to swallow us whole if we give it a chance. Though some people believe everyone gets to heaven no matter what they do, with or without Jesus, the Bible simply does not agree. Nevertheless, all have sinned—that includes me.

Thankfully, Jesus died for each of us. Accepting Him is accepting forgiveness of sin. Or, the one and true *atonement*, as the Bible calls it, through our Saviour Jesus:

> *Nor is there salvation in any other, for there is no other name under heaven given among men by which we must be saved.* —*Acts 4:12*

> *Jesus said to him, "I am the way, the truth, and the life. No one comes to the Father except through Me.* —*John 14:6*

All Roads Lead to The Cross, Continued

It is notable that among the people in the Exodus, the men in each of the twelve tribes who were twenty years of age or older, and who were able to go to war, were counted and recorded in Numbers Chapter 1 and 2. Everything in the Bible is there for a reason. The twelve tribes were encamped in groups of three to the east, south, west and north of the Tabernacle.

When you add up the numbers of each of the groups of three tribes, the pattern of their encampment formed the pattern of the cross in an aerial view. The east encampment was the largest and was located at the foot of the pattern of the cross.[28]

You don't have to understand all the details of the Mosaic Tabernacle to be able to obtain a personal relationship with Jesus. The Old Testament is basically a foreshadowing of the New Testament; it foreshadows Jesus and the work of the cross. You can't underestimate the importance of what was accomplished by

---

28 Torturing and killing people by means of nailing them to a cross was something invented by the Romans many years after the tabernacle days of the Exodus.

Jesus dying on the cross for our sins. In Biblical terminology, it is called the atonement.

The book of Hebrews provides an overview of the Old Testament and how it relates to the New Testament. Hebrews Chapter 9 explains the ordinances that were part of the Mosaic Tabernacle. There is no remission of sins without the shedding of blood. Jesus paid the ultimate price to enable us to receive forgiveness of our sins. He willingly shed his blood on the cross. (Read the entire chapter 9 of Hebrews).

> *He (Jesus Christ) has appeared to put away sin by the sacrifice of Himself. And as it is appointed for men to die once, but after this the judgement, so Christ was offered once to bear the sins of many. — Hebrews 9:26b-28a*

The Word of God as Outlined in Psalm 119

Psalm 119 speaks in first person, present tense. Each eight-verse section outlines why the Word of God is so important. I did some counting, and the word "Your," with a capital "Y," referring to God, appears 210 times in Psalm 119.

- "Your word" in 39 verses
- "Your law" in 23 verses
- "Your statutes" in 22 verses
- "Your precepts" in 20 verses
- "Your commandments" in 20 verses
- "Your testimonies" in 20 verses

The aspects of the Lord's character and what He does for us, are referred to throughout chapter 119, including:

- Your righteous judgements
- Your ways

- Your wonderful works
- Your righteousness
- Your lovingkindness
- Your ordinances
- Your name
- Your favour
- Your mercy
- Your faithfulness
- Your custom
- Your ordinances
- Your justice
- Your salvation

Study and meditate on Psalm 119. It will give you a hunger for the Word of God.

The Parable of the Sower

In one of the Bible studies I attended, I heard an explanation of why some parables are repeated, with each account being slightly different. An illustration was given of an automobile accident scene: if four people at an intersection—one on each corner—witness a car accident, you get the same account of what happened, but with slightly different details—depending on their viewpoint and perspective. So, if you want to get an overall picture of what happened, you cannot simply read one of the statements—you must read them all.

The Parable of the Sower is a key for helping us understanding the other parables. The verses explaining this parable are repeated in the books of Matthew, Mark, and Luke. It shows the progression of firstly, hearing the Word; then understanding and receiving the Word; and ultimately, keeping the Word. The seed is the same throughout, but it is sown into different soils.

At the beginning of the explanation of the parable in Matthew 13:18 (KJV), Jesus says: "Hear ye therefore the parable of the sower." We need to not only listen; but *hear* the Word of God. And in context. The verses before and after the key verses should be read because they are part of your understanding, receiving, and keeping. Also, it does not say "having heard," but "hearing." We must continue listening. We must continue hearing. Faith develops through active hearing.

Hear (listen to)
the word of God,
...understand it,
...receive it,
and keep it.

But he that received seed into the good ground is he that heareth the word, and understandeth it; which also beareth fruit, and bringeth forth, some a hundredfold, some sixty, some thirty.
— Matthew 13:23

And these are they which are sown on good ground; such as hear the word, and receive it, and bring forth fruit, some thirtyfold, some sixty, and some a hundred.
— Mark 4:20

But that on the good ground are they, which in an honest and good heart, having heard the word, keep it, and bring forth fruit with patience.
— Luke 8:15

He that hath ears to hear, let him hear.
— Matthew 13:9 — Mark 4:9 — Luke 8:8

The Parable of the Sower

The Dominion of Canada and Psalm 72:8

Two major Canadian milestones were the Centennial Year in 1967 and Canada's 150-year anniversary in 2017. With metrification being put in place in the mid-1980s, to be technically correct, 1967 was a milestone and 2017 was a 1.6 kilometer-stone... No, I suppose it doesn't have quite the same ring to it... I'll stick with calling them both milestone events.

As stated earlier, in 1967, my Centennial project (as a fifteen-year-old), was to read the Bible, cover to cover. Reading the Bible, I believed, was something I would only do once in my life. I believe I was prompted to make this goal as a result of Mr. Hertzsprung's prayers, and since, I have completed multiple trips through the Bible.

In mid-June of 2017, much of my time in prayer was focused on the upcoming 150th anniversary of Canada's confederation. I thought about how I had such an appropriate project in 1967 to read the Bible, and now, fifty years later, I was searching for a calligraphy project to commemorate the event. It was not just a Canadian milestone, it was also my fifty-mile marker, signifying fifty years of reading the Bible.

On June 29th, 2017, I went to bed thinking about what I could plan to do on July 1st. That night, in a dream, I visualized a map of Canada on which I had written the verse of Psalm 72:8 over the map, in a fish pattern. The fish pattern was formed by the words themselves, which had been my original idea for the border of the Psalm 91 scroll I did in 1975.

I woke up on the morning of June 30th, found a Canada Map in a tote of old homeschool material, and traced the outline of the map on an 8.5"x 11" sheet of paper. Then I made a photocopy of it and pencilled the words across the map. As I was doing this, I realized the letters could actually touch every province and territory, so I adjusted the fish pattern to do just that. It is amazing how the words of Psalm 72:8, written over Canada's geography, actually fit the description of the verse.

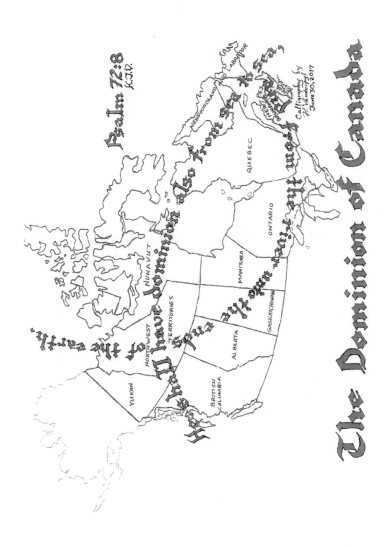

Earlier that month, I learned that the Bible League had published a book commemorating Canada's 150th anniversary of
Confederation. I had ordered a copy of the book, and it arrived
on July 4th. It explains how the name of our country was decided:

> On September 1, 1864, delegates from the British
> Colonies of New Brunswick, Nova Scotia and Prince
> Edward Island met in Charlottetown to discuss a poten-
> tial Maritime Union of those colonies into a new nation.
> They were joined by delegates from Upper and Lower
> Canada who had asked to attend. The original inten-
> tion of the meeting was broadened, and it was decided
> a confederation of colonies was in the best interest of
> British North America and the British Empire.
>
> At the end of the Conference, these Fathers of
> Confederation had already determined they were going
> to call this new nation "Canada." But they debated
> about how it would be designated. Because they did not
> want to sever ties with the British Monarchy, Canada
> could not be called a republic. While some wanted to
> designate it as the Kingdom of Canada, the Conference
> decided against that in fear it would enflame the
> Americans who held residual resentment toward
> the British Crown from the time of the American
> Revolution and who well remembered the War of
> 1812. Unable to make a final decision, they completed
> their deliberations for the evening and the participants
> returned back to their lodging.
>
> One of the delegates was Sir Leonard Tilley, who
> had entered politics years earlier, serving as Lieutenant
> Governor and then later as the Premier of New
> Brunswick. Tilley devoted his life to seeing this nation
> formed under the power of God, so much so that at

the end of his life he told his family to put on his grave
"his trust was in Jesus."[25] (ref. Michael Clarke, Canada:
Portraits of Faith (Chilliwack, BC: Reel to Real, 1998),
p61) He wanted them to know that Jesus had been the
true source of his success and the Power that influenced
his life.

Sir Leonard Tilley got up the following morning
of the Conference with the same mandate that all the
delegates had: what are we going to call this nation of
Canada? That morning he was reading scripture, which
had been his habit since childhood. He was beside his
bed when he read, "He shall have dominion also from
sea to sea and from the river unto the ends of the
earth" (Psalm 72:8 KJV). He stopped reading because
he had read far enough. He rose from his knees and
returned to the Confederation Conference. Telling the
delegates that he was so convinced Canada should be
one Dominion under God, he recommended from that
point on, the nation should be named "The Dominion
of Canada."[26] (William S. Wallace, The Encyclopedia
of Canada, Vol. II (Toronto: University Associates of
Canada, 1948), p223) The Fathers of Confederation
agreed and expressed their desire that God would have
dominion from sea to sea and from the river to the ends
of the earth.

(*One Dominion: Celebrating Canada - Prepared for a Purpose*,
by Bob Beasley and Paul Richardson, Bible League Canada,
copyright 2017—used with permission)

I did not know that portion of our Canadian history until I read
the book from the Bible League Canada, four days after completing my Psalm 72:8 Canadian geo-calligraphy project. It amazed

me how my calligraphy map dove-tailed with the book's history. We were founded as a Godly nation based on scripture taken from the Bible. That is our heritage. The Bible League Canada book goes on to state:

> It is our belief that in the naming of Canada that day we received both our national mandate as well as our international mandate: our national mandate seeing God have dominion "from sea to sea" (Psalm 72:8a KJV), and our international mandate seeing God have dominion "unto the ends of the earth." (Psalm 72:8b, KJV)

I am proud of our heritage as Canadians—that we are a nation founded on Godly principles. I pray that we will not stray (further) from our roots, but maintain our heritage based on the scriptures. This applies to each and every province and territory.

My calligraphy verse is written so that it has letters touching every province and territory on the map—sea to sea, Pacific to Atlantic, and from the St. Lawrence Seaway to the Arctic, and the North Pole—unto the ends of the earth. In the margin of one of my Bibles it clarifies that "dominion" refers to "sovereignty." Also note that "ends of the earth" is plural. Canada has a worldwide calling—an international mandate.

The message on the Jesus Elevator also serves as a reminder of a larger vision for Canada. It talks about 'the whole world'. Canada has been blessed as a unique nation with a unique place in history for the present, and in the future. Think of the far-reaching calling on the nation of Canada—it was named the Dominion of Canada for a reason. We are living in exciting times.

It was very special for me to wake up on the morning of June 30, 2017 visualizing Psalm 72 verse 8 on a map of Canada—the day before the 150th Anniversary of confederation. We can build on our past experiences and, with Jesus, we can build on our future.

It is my prayer that everyone will follow the example of Sir Leonard Tilley; and begin each day by reading part of your Bible. And if the mornings don't suit you well, choose another time slot. Or, better yet, treat it like your smart phone and check your Bible throughout the day for new messages.

Protection and Encouragement from the Scriptures

I encourage you to find the scriptures that minister to your situation, that are relevant to you. Write them out and read them, study them, and enjoy the wisdom in the Word. Understand, receive, and keep the life changing message of the Bible.

Scriptures which ministered to me and others I shared them with, include:

- "No weapon that is formed against thee shall prosper" –from Isaiah 54:17, is written as per the King James Version and compared with The Living Bible. I wrote this calligraphy in 1987, and shared copies of it with Christian leaders who were facing attacks against their Biblical beliefs.

- "For God has not given us a spirit of fear, but of power and of love and of a sound mind." –2 Tim 1:7. This is a verse that ministered to me just after I committed my life to serving Jesus. I was walking into a Bible study, but I had been putting off writing an apology letter to my Dad. I went into an adjacent room instead and started writing the letter. One of the leaders saw me and shared this verse to help me deal with the task of writing that letter. I finished it there in that room. When you focus on what the scriptures say, it empowers you to do the task at hand. We should not be overly anxious.

• "Trust in the LORD with all thine heart; and lean not unto thine own understanding. In all thy ways acknowledge him, and he shall direct thy paths." —Proverbs 3:5,6 (KJV). This is a verse that helped me in keeping a right perspective when making many important decisions. I didn't always fully trust the Lord, but I sure tried to. Christians are not perfect, but we can follow instructions and trust in the teachings of God's Word the Bible.

No weapon that is formed against thee shall prosper; and every tongue that shall rise against thee in judgement thou shalt condemn. This is the heritage of the servants of the Lord, and their righteousness is of me, saith the Lord.
                              -Isaiah 54:17 KJV

But in that coming day, no weapon turned against you shall succeed, and you will have justice against every courtroom lie. This is the heritage of the servants of the Lord. This is the blessing I have given you, says the Lord.
                              -Isaiah 54:17 TLB

For God has not given us a spirit of fear, but of power and of love and of a sound mind.
—2 Timothy 1:7 (NKJV)

Be anxious for nothing, but in everything by prayer and supplication, with thanksgiving, let your requests be made known to God; and the peace of God, which surpasses all understanding, will guard your hearts and minds through Christ Jesus.
—Phil. 4:6,7 (NKJV)

When you lie down, you will not be afraid;
Yes, you will lie down and your sleep will be sweet.

Do not be afraid of sudden terror,
Nor of trouble from the wicked when it comes;

For the LORD will be your confidence,
And will keep your foot from being caught.

—Proverbs 3:24-26 (NKJV)

I have noticed it is easy for me to dwell on the negative side of a difficult situation or set of circumstances. A pessimist may see a glass half empty instead of half full—an engineer will tell you that you have fifty percent more glass than needed. It is all a matter of perspective. Washing in the "water of the word" gives you a better perspective.

Unfortunately, most of us know someone who has committed suicide. Hotel rooms are often places where negative thoughts, including suicidal thoughts, are mulled over. On the following four pages is a copy of the "Where to Find Help When" index from one of the Gideons Bibles I have. It is reproduced here with their permission.

Answers for Life's Big Questions

Every person wrestles with life's big questions and wants to know some answers. Listed here are the five big questions people ask, with Scripture passages that help answer them.

ORIGINS — Where did we come from?

John 1:1–13	p. 158
Acts 17:22–31	p. 234
Colossians 1:15–20	p. 347
Revelation 4:11	p. 432
Psalm 33	p. 482
Psalm 148:1–6	p. 590

PURPOSE — Why are we here? Is there any real purpose in life and, if so, how can I find it?

John 15:1–17	p. 188
Ephesians 1:3–14	p. 332
Ephesians 2:1–10	p. 333

CONNECTION / COMMUNITY — Where and how can I connect with other people in meaningful relationships?

Acts 2:41–47	p. 204
1 Corinthians 12:12–26	p. 298
Ephesians 2:11–22	p. 334
Hebrews 10:19–25	p. 398

HOPE — Is there any real hope for us and for the future?

Romans 5:1–11	p. 263
Romans 8:18–39	p. 268
Romans 15:4, 13	p. 279
1 Peter 1:17–21	p. 403

DESTINY — Is this life all there is, or is there something beyond the grave?

Matthew 24:1–35	p. 47
Matthew 25:31–46	p. 51
John 14:1–31	p. 187
1 Corinthians 15:12–58	p. 302
1 Peter 1:3–9	p. 402
2 Peter 3:1–13	p. 411
Revelation 20:1 – 22:6	p. 400

5

Where to Find Help When ...

		PAGE			PAGE
Addicted	John 8:34-36	175	**Distressed**	Romans 8:28–39	268
	James 1:13-15	396	**or Troubled**	2 Cor. 4:8–9, 16–18	311
				Psalm 9:9–10	462
Afraid	Mark 4:35–41	68		Psalm 50:14–15	500
	Psalm 56:3–4,10–11	504			
			Doubting	Mark 9:23–24	79
Attacked	Luke 23:34	154		John 20:24–29	198
	Psalm 35:1–2	484		Psalm 53:1	502
	Psalm 54:1–4	502			
			Facing	John 3:16	162
Bereaved /	1 Thess. 4:13–18	355	**Death**	John 14:1–3	187
Brokenhearted	Revelation 21:3–5	451		Revelation 21:4	451
	Psalm 147:3	589		Psalm 23:4	474
Bitter or	Matthew 7:1–5	13			
Critical	Romans 14:10–13	278	**Failure**	Hebrews 4:14–16	381
	1 Corinthians 4:5	287	**Comes**	Psalm 73:26	521
	Psalm 73:21–25	521		Psalm 77	524
				Psalm 84:11	534
Choosing	Romans 12:1–2	275			
a Career	James 1:5–8	396	**Faith is**	Matthew 8:5–13	14
			Weak	Luke 12:22–31	130
Conscious	Luke 15:11–24	136		Hebrews 11	390
of Sin	1 John 1:5–10	414			
	Psalm 51	500	**Far from**	Luke 19:10	143
	Psalm 103:12	549	**God**	James 4:8	400
				Psalm 42:5–11	492
Considering	Mark 10:1–12	80		Psalm 107:4–9	556
Divorce	Romans 7:2–3	266		Psalm 139:1–18	583
	Psalm 86:1, 7	535		Psalm 145:18	587
Considering	Matthew 19:4–6	37	**Feeling**	1 Cor. 1:25–31	284
Marriage	Ephesians 5:22–33	338	**Inadequate**	2 Cor. 12:9–10	320
	Hebrews 13:4	394		Philippians 4:12–13	345
				Psalm 138:8	582
Contemplating	Romans 12:17–19	276			
Revenge	1 Thess. 5:15	356	**Friends Fail**	Luke 17:3–4	139
	1 Peter 2:21–23	405		2 Timothy 4:16–18	371
				Psalm 27:10–14	477
Desperate	Psalm 55:16, 17, 22	503		Psalm 41	491
	Psalm 61:1–3	508			
	Psalm 62:1–2	509	**Gambling**	1 Timothy 6:10	365
	Psalm 94:18, 19, 22	543		Hebrews 13:5	379
	Psalm 121:1–2, 7–8	574			

Where to Find Help When ...

		PAGE			PAGE
Ill or in Pain	2 Cor. 12:9–10	320	**Sleepless**	Matthew 11:28	20
	James 5:14–16	401		Psalm 3	458
	Psalm 38:3–10	488		Psalm 4:8	459
	Psalm 69:29–30	517			
	Psalm 103:1–4	549	**Sorrowful**	Psalm 23	474
				Psalm 34:18	484
In Danger or	Mark 4:37–41	68		Psalm 147:3	589
Threatened	1 Peter 3:13–14	406			
	Psalm 27:1–3	477	**Tempted by**	1 Corinthians 10:31	296
	Psalm 118:6–9	565	**Drink Abuse**	Ephesians 5:18	337
				1 Thess. 5:6–8	356
Insulted or	1 Peter 2:20–23	405			
Intimidated	Psalm 3	458	**Tempted by**	John 8:34–36	175
	Psalm 55:20–22	503	**Drug Abuse**	Psa.139:1–5, 13–14	583
				1 Cor. 6:12, 19–20	289
Just Retired	Matthew 6:33–34	13			
	Philippians 4:12–13	345	**Tempted to**	1 Cor. 6:9–10, 13	289
			Commit	Galatians 5:19–23	330
Lonely	Revelation 3:20	431	**Sexual**	1 Thess. 4:3–7	354
	Psalm 23	474	**Immorality**		
	1 Peter 5:7	408			
	Hebrews 13:5,6	394	**Tempted to**	1 Cor. 3:16–17	286
			Commit	Psalm 42:5–11	493
Looking for	Colossians 3:17, 23	350	**Suicide**	Psa.139:1–5, 13–14	583
a Job	Psalm 71:3	518			
			Tempted	Galatians 5:26	330
Needing	John 3:16	162	**to Envy**	Philippians 4:11	345
Forgiveness	1 John 1:9	414		James 3:14–18	399
Needing	Romans 12:1–2	275	**Tempted**	John 8:44	175
Guidance	Psalm 32:8–10	482	**to Lie**	Ephesians 4:25	336
				Revelation 21:8	451
Needing	John 14:27	188			
Peace	Romans 5:1–2	263	**Tempted to**	Romans 13:9–10	279
	Philippians 4:4–7	344	**Steal**	Ephesians 4:28	337
				Hebrews 13:5	394
Praying	Luke 11:1–13	126			
	John 14:12–14	187	**Thankful**	2 Corinthians 2:14	309
	James 5:13, 16	401		Ephesians 5:18–20	337
	1 John 5:14–15	419		Psalm 92:1–5	542
	Psalm 66:17, 20	511		Psalm 100	547

Tips for Reading the Bible

1. **Pray,** ask the Helper, the Holy Spirit to assist you with your reading, to help you understand and apply it.

    But the Helper, the Holy Spirit, whom the Father will send in My name, He will teach you all things, and bring to your remembrance all things that I said to you. – John 14:26

2. **Plan,** have a daily reading plan, and schedule it. A good suggestion is to read some scriptures out of the Old Testament, and some out of the New Testament every day. Using a smartphone app such as YouVersion helps to facilitate daily reading.

    All Scripture is given by inspiration of God, and is profitable for doctrine, for reproof, for correction, for instruction in righteousness, that the man of God may be complete, thoroughly equipped for every good work. —2 Timothy 3:16,17

3. **Take notes,** and/or highlight and mark with an asterisk or an arrow to emphasize what is important to you and your circumstances, so that you don't forget.

    Then He said to them "Therefore every scribe instructed concerning the kingdom of heaven is like a householder who brings out of his treasure things new and old. –Matthew 13:52

4. **Use a Concordance** and check the cross-references. There are Bible smartphone apps that assist with this. We are blessed with an abundance of study aids.

5. **Meditate on the Word.** Study and contemplate what the Word is saying and how you can apply it. Listening is the other half of talking or reading.

   Cease listening to instruction my son, and you will stray from the words of knowledge. —Proverbs 19:27

6. **Mind on Task:** Stop, refocus, get your mind on task. Try to not be distracted, for instance you could say: "Okay, this is the last thing I'm checking in my email for a while. I'm going to go and read my Bible." As well, you can also pray for God to help you focus. (Feed your focus, starve your distraction.)

   Finally, brethren, whatever things are true, whatever things are noble, whatever things are just, whatever things are pure, whatever things are lovely, whatever things are of good report, if there is any virtue and if there is anything praiseworthy—meditate on these things. —Philippians 4:8

Reading and memorizing God's Word is facilitated by putting it on display. Posting it on your fridge, making a plaque and hanging it where it is noticed—helps you in daily reading and memorizing. *Get into the Word of God, and the Word of God will get into you.* Pray before reading the Bible; and ask for daily bread. There is power in the word:

*So shall My word be that goes forth from My mouth;
It shall not return to Me void, but it shall accomplish
what I please, and it shall prosper in the thing for which
I sent it. —Isaiah 55:11*

*For I am not ashamed of the gospel of Christ, for it is the
power of God to salvation for everyone who believes, for
the Jew first and also for the Greek. –Romans 1:16*

*Be diligent to present yourself approved to God, a
worker who does not need to be ashamed, rightly divid-
ing the word of truth. —2 Timothy 2:15*

*but grow in the grace and knowledge of our Lord and
Savior Jesus Christ. To Him be the glory both now and
forever. Amen. —2 Peter 3:18*

Romans Road to Salvation

When my Dad was in the hospital facing major surgery (a qua-
druple heart bypass with other complications), I wrote a list of
scriptures along with partial quotes to assist him in reading his
Bible. I explained the salvation message (the Gospel) and prayed—
out loud—that he would understand and receive it. Here is what
I wrote:

1. <u>**All have sinned.**</u>
   Romans 3: 23 ...for all have sinned and fall short of the
   glory of God,
   Romans 3: 10-19 ...There is none righteous, no, not one; ...
   Mark 7: 20-23 ...What comes out of a man, that defiles a
   man. ...

Romans 5: 12 ...Therefore, just as through one man sin entered the world, and death through sin, and thus death spread to all men, because all sinned— ...

2. **The wages of sin is death.**
    Romans 6: 23 ...For the wages of sin is death, but the gift of God is eternal life....
    Revelation 20: 11-15 ...And anyone not found written in the Book of Life was cast into the lake of fire.

3. **Jesus Christ died for our salvation.**
    Romans 5: 6-8 ...while we were still sinners, Christ died for us
    I Peter 2: 21-25 ...who Himself bore our sins in His own body on the tree, ...
    I Peter 1: 18-25 ...through the word of God which lives and abides forever, ...
    John 3: 16 ...For God so loved the world that He gave His only begotten Son, that....
    Titus 3: 5-9 .... not by works .... but according to His mercy He saved us, ...
    Ephesians 2: 8-10 ...For by grace you have been saved through faith...

4. **Repent and receive Jesus Christ as your Lord and Saviour.**
    Romans 10: 8-13 ...if you confess with your mouth the Lord Jesus and believe in your heart that God has raised Him from the dead, you will be saved.
    Revelation 3: 20-21 ... Behold, I stand at the door and knock. If anyone hears my voice...
    I John 5: 5-6 ...Who is he who overcomes the world, but he who believes that Jesus is the Son of God?

The greatest gift you can receive is the gift of eternal life through accepting Jesus Christ as your Lord and Saviour.

My Dad, who was a heavy smoker, recovered from the surgery, but the doctors could only do a triple bypass due to the damage that had already been done. He lived for several months before he passed away. I knew he read his Bible, but whether or not he received Jesus as his Lord, I'm not sure. I do know, however, that God is a just God.

> For the grace of God that brings salvation has appeared to all men, teaching us that, denying ungodliness and worldly lusts, we should live soberly, righteously, and godly in the present age, looking for the blessed hope and glorious appearing of our great God and Savior Jesus Christ. —Titus 2:11-13

My Dad did not attend church, but there was one pastor that had contact with him. When Dad passed away, we met the pastor for the first time, at his office. I noticed that a copy of the Psalm 91 scroll, which was the same as the one hanging in The Hiding Place, was hanging prominently on display in his office. The pastor had not known the connection, but God did.

Salvation is a heart issue. It is not based on religious works. In all your getting, get understanding—understanding of God's Word and it will give health to our entire being. Read Proverbs 4:1-27, the entire chapter, and see the context of these verses:

> Wisdom is the principal thing; therefore get wisdom. And in all your getting, get understanding. — Proverbs 4:7

*My son, give attention to my words; Incline your ear
to my sayings. Do not let them depart from your eyes;
Keep them in the midst of your heart; For they are life
to those who find them, and health to all their flesh. —
Proverbs 4:20-22*

Some people believe that people who die become reincarnated.
The Bible does not say that. We will all face judgement and our
ultimate destination is either heaven or hell. We lose loved family
members and friends when they die, and we grieve for them.
Things like butterflies can remind us of our loved ones. Rainbows
were created by God as a sign to remind us that a catastrophic
flood, like what killed all the people on earth except for Noah and
his family, would not reoccur.

Flowers, butterflies, and nature may serve to remind us of
people we miss, and that can be part of the grieving process. We
relate to them in our thoughts, but reincarnation is not biblical.

What about the person in the Amazon wilderness, or in other
remote places, who has never read a Bible?

*For the grace of God that brings salvation has appeared
to all men, —Titus 2:11*

For as he thinks in his heart, so is he. —Proverbs 23:7a

God is a just God. We have our own definition of fairness, but
we are finite, and God is infinite. You cannot use that which is finite
to fully comprehend the infinite. His character is much better than
ours; we serve a good God. The Bible gives us the good news of
redemption. But we must be born-again in our inner being, in our
spirit. We need to repent and accept Jesus as our Lord.

Do you have absolute assurance that when you die you will go
to heaven?

And this is the testimony: that God has given us eternal life, and this life is in His Son. He who has the Son has life; he who does not have the Son of God does not have life. These things I have written to you who believe in the name of the Son of God, that you may know that you have eternal life, and that you may continue to believe in the name of the Son of God. —1 John 5: 11-13

And this is the testimony: that God has given us eternal life, and this life is in His Son.

He who has the Son has life; he who does not have the Son of God does not have life.

These things I have written to you who believe in the name of the Son of God, that you may know that you have eternal life, and that you may continue to believe in the name of the Son of God.

~ 1 John 5:11-13 (NKJV)

It is my prayer that somehow, maybe by reading this book, everyone is encouraged to read the Bible daily—and most importantly, that each of you receive Jesus as your Lord and Saviour. Make Him the Lord of your life. Salvation only comes but one way: through faith in Jesus Christ, and Him alone.

Choosing to side with God's Word is an ongoing challenge. It is something you do daily, in almost every circumstance. You need to choose Him as your LORD and Saviour, and as the head of your household. See Joshua 24:15.

It has been my intention to follow the right path, but sometimes I find myself going in the wrong direction. Then I realize: no matter how long I travel in the wrong direction, I can always turn around. It is my direction, not my intention, that determines whether or not I get to Heaven.

Jesus loves me, yes I know, for the Bible tells me so. That applies to each one of us, because we have an infinite, loving Creator, and he wants all of us to come to repentance at the foot of the cross.

For God so loved the world that He gave His only begotten Son, that whoever believes in Him should not perish but have everlasting life. For God did not send His Son into the world to condemn the world, but that the world through Him might be saved. He who believes in Him is not condemned; but he who does not believe is condemned already, because he has not believed in the name of the only begotten Son of God. —John 3:16-18

The grass withereth, the flower fadeth: but the word of our God shall stand forever.

-Isaiah 40:8 (KJV)